DIGGING
into
ARCHAEOLOGY

Hands-On • Minds-On Unit Study

Written by Julie Coan

Illustrated by Ellisa C. Holder

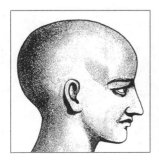

© 1999
CRITICAL THINKING BOOKS & SOFTWARE
www.criticalthinking.com
P.O. Box 448 • Pacific Grove • CA 93950-0448
Phone 800-458-4849 • FAX 831-393-3277
ISBN 0-89455-718-1
Printed in the United States of America

TABLE OF CONTENTS

UNIT 4 WHAT IS A CIVILIZATION?

UNIT 5 ARCHAEOLOGICAL DATING METHODS

EXTENSION ACTIVITIES

ANSWERS

YOU SHOULD USE THIS BOOK IF...

- your students groan every time you ask them to take out their social studies or history books
- you taught a whole chapter on culture and civilization, and only the two "brains" in the class passed the final test
- you need hands-on, minds-on activities for your students, but you don't have time to prepare them
- you get blank stares when you ask students to tell you what culture is
- you catch one of your students sleeping in the middle of your history lecture
- you feel that concepts like specialization of labor and domestication are too difficult for your students to understand
- you're tired of asking your students to write about the civilization of Ancient Greece and getting answers like, "It was neat"
- your students come to your class with a wide variety of academic experiences
- you are looking for a unique approach to teaching traditional material
- you are bored with your textbook
- you want to expand your students' abilities to think and reason

THIS BOOK WILL PROVIDE...

- activities that are both hands-on and minds-on

- activities that are based on the constructivist approach, which equalizes students with a variety of academic experiences

- practice in the development of the critical thinking skills of synthesizing, analyzing, evaluating, hypothesizing, application, and deductive and inductive reasoning

- a catalyst for enthusiasm (and maybe even excitement) during the learning of social studies

- lessons which cover concepts that are critical to the understanding of history

- a chance for students to look at history through the eyes of an archaeologist

- concept-oriented lessons, rather than lessons based on rote memorization of facts

Why Teach Archaeology?

If a teacher were to rate a subject's importance by the number of pages allotted to it in the textbook, then archaeology would be one of the least important subjects in the teacher's curriculum. In most textbooks, archaeology is discussed on a page or two. There is a temptation to skip it altogether and go directly to the "important" material, but this would be a mistake. Archaeology provides the key to understanding everything that we know about human civilization. Studying the world's civilizations without understanding archaeology is like being given the pieces of a jigsaw puzzle and trying to put it together without any idea of what the finished picture is supposed to look like.

Archaeology forms the basis for how we came to know about the civilizations that preceded ours. Archaeologists dig up long buried towns and villages. They study the broken remains of buildings, streets, pottery, carvings, and anything else that was left behind, in order to learn about the life-style and culture of ancient people. They even study the contents of the town's garbage heap. By studying artifacts and other objects found at a dig site, archaeologists are able to describe a civilization in amazing detail. They can decipher the development of its written language. They can tell about its political and economic structure. They can determine the extent of its trade and interaction with other cultures. They are able to identify the tenets of its religion and note the effect it had on the lives of its people. They can even ascertain its familial organization and deduce its cultural mores.

The information that archaeologists discover provides many pieces of the jigsaw puzzle that we ask students to study. Teachers want students to understand the larger picture of which all of this information is a part. The hieroglyphics in Egypt, the cuneiform in Sumeria, and the characters of Chinese writing are the pieces of the jigsaw puzzle, but they form a larger picture that says that human beings need to communicate in writing. The pyramids of Egypt, the ziggurats in Mesopotamia, the temples in South America, and the Great Wall of China are the pieces of the jigsaw puzzle, but they form a larger picture that says that human leaders need to show their power by building large physical structures as a monument

to their greatness. Egyptians grew wheat, Mesopotamians grew barley, the Chinese grew rice. These are the pieces of the jigsaw puzzle, but the larger picture shows that they followed the same path from a hunter-gatherer society to an agricultural society. Every culture has a religion of some kind. Every culture creates shelters from the weather, tools, and methods of cooking food.

The complete picture becomes very clear. Although cultures differ greatly around the world, there are more similarities than there are differences. All archaeologists base their interpretations and assumptions about human artifacts not on those things that are unique, but on those things that are common to every member of the human race.

By studying many civilizations, students can begin to understand patterns common to all cultures. They can identify similar stages of development. When students study other civilizations, they are really learning about themselves.

Critical Thinking

The most important thing teachers can teach students is not math, or science, or reading. The most important thing teachers can teach their students is how to think. Critical thinking skills are the essence of good education. They are the skeleton on which the muscles and organs are supported. Teaching a child to think critically requires the use of several important teaching techniques. The first technique is to focus on the teaching of concepts rather than facts. The second technique is to design the lesson so that it includes skills that enhance critical thinking. The third technique is to follow a lesson format that allows multiple opportunities to learn each concept.

Technique 1

Learning consists of two parts—knowing and understanding. One is useless without the other. If we teach students only to know without teaching them to understand, then we will have a generation of students who can talk about things, but cannot make connections to other things and, therefore, cannot advance their ideas to their next level. They will have been robbed of the ability to create something new from what they have learned.

The optimal goal of education is to teach both knowledge and understanding. Knowledge comes from learning facts, and understanding comes from applying concepts. Facts are isolated pieces of information. Concepts are ideas which encompass both facts and the processes and ideas that link those facts. For example, Earth has a 24-hour day—this is a fact. Students can memorize it and repeat it back, but they will not understand why Earth's day lasts for 24 hours. The length of a planet's day is based on the speed of its rotation on its axis—this is a concept. Given both fact and concept, students will know the length of Earth's day. They will understand why it lasts for 24 hours and why every planet has its own particular length of day.

Lessons should focus on a concept rather than a fact. As the lesson progresses, students are presented with a series of facts and guided into finding the connecting threads. By the end of the lesson, students should know the facts and understand the concept of the lesson.

Technique 2

Critical thinking cannot be taught by asking students to read a textbook and answer questions whose answers are stated in the text. Students must be enticed into connecting the new information they receive to what they already know (either through reading or teacher lecture). They must demonstrate that connection by creating something that is a combination of what they have learned and what they already knew. If we teach students only facts and do not teach them how to use those facts, then we have truly failed to educate.

Critical thinking is habit-forming. As soon as students are repeatedly required to use these skills, they will begin to use them reflexively. Once teachers begin to teach these skills, they will also find that they are easier to incorporate into their lessons on a regular basis.

In the repertoire of a student who is taught to think critically are the abilities to observe, apply, organize, analyze, classify, compare and contrast, synthesize, evaluate, deduce, generalize, hypothesize, and predict. All of these skills allow students to move beyond the memorization of facts. These are the skills that truly expand the students' minds and allow them to become problem solvers and critical thinkers. The

lessons in this book provide generous practice in the critical thinking skills on the following list.

- Application exercises require students to make use of what they have learned and apply the original information to a different situation.

- Analysis exercises require students to take apart what is known. They will separate the parts, compare, contrast, and classify.

- Synthesis exercises require students to put together new information with information that they already know and create a new product or idea.

- Evaluation exercises require students to make a judgment or form an opinion about the information presented to them.

- Deductive Reasoning exercises require students to make reasonable conclusions about a specific item or circumstance using general information.

- Inductive Reasoning exercises require students to make generalizations from a collection of specific facts.

- Hypothesizing exercises require students to create a reasonable theory to explain why something occurred.

Technique 3

A lesson format with multiple learning opportunities is essential to quality instruction. In each step of the lesson, the same concept is presented and practiced in a similar mode. At each step, the student takes an increasingly autonomic role until at the final stage, the student is able to demonstrate the concept independently. The lessons in this book follow this format.

The first step of each lesson is "Introducing the Lesson." In the introduction, the teacher focuses the learner on the concept of the lesson. This can be done in a variety of ways, including simply telling the students what concept they are going to study during the lesson. If the topic is difficult and somewhat unusual, the constructivist approach is recommended. This approach begins by presenting an activity that provides all students with a common experience on which they are then asked to construct their own interpretation.

"Acquiring Information" is an optional step that

follows the introduction to the lesson. During "Acquiring Information," the teacher presents the concept in detail to the students. At this point, the students are presented only with information. They may be asked at various points to contribute information they already know, but they are not expected to practice the concept in any way.

The next step is "Guided Practice." During "Guided Practice," students begin to practice the concept. At this point, the students will not yet fully understand the concept. They are not expected to be able to complete this activity on their own. They will complete this activity either with the teacher or with the teacher's repeated assistance and guidance.

After "Guided Practice," students are given "Independent Practice." During this time, students will again practice the concept that is targeted in the lesson. Students are expected to be able to nearly complete this activity on their own. This is a chance for each student to find out if there are still questions about the concept. The teacher is still involved in this part of the lesson as a reference to answer specific individual questions.

Some lessons include "Closure." The student completes an activity without any assistance from the teacher. This activity is a demonstration by the student that he/she has mastered the concept that was taught during the lesson. It allows the teacher to make sure that each student understood the concept and to provide remedial instruction, if necessary.

UNIT 1
THE ARCHAEOLOGICAL RECORD

Chapter 1
Deeper is Older

Background Information

Stratigraphy and the principle of superposition are important concepts in archaeology, and it is important for students to have a firm understanding of them. However, it is not important that students learn the words *stratigraphy* and *superposition*, only that they understand their meaning. In fact, trying to teach complex vocabulary may interfere with conceptual learning.

Stratigraphy is the study of stratified, or layered, earth. These layers are called "strata." (Use, and encourage students to use, the term "strata" when discussing the lesson. The term "stratum" is singular [one layer], "strata" is plural [several layers].) Strata are usually arranged in horizontal layers like a cake (icing, cake, icing, cake, etc.). Archaeologists study these layers (strata) in relation to the objects they find. Objects that are found in the same stratum at the same location are probably from the same period of time. However, a vase that is uncovered three feet below the surface in China is not necessarily more recent than a vase uncovered six feet below the surface in Brazil. Dirt and other debris accumulate at vastly different rates in different areas.

Superposition follows this principle: given any undisturbed strata, the bottom layer is the oldest and the layers above it are successively younger. Hence, the deeper you dig in the soil, the older the objects that are uncovered will be. Objects uncovered nearest the surface are generally the most recent. Of course, there are exceptions, but archaeologists use this principle as a basic guideline and so will these lessons.

Neither stratigraphy nor superposition can provide archaeologists with an absolute age of an object, but they can give them an idea of relative age.

(Lessons on more exact dating methods can be found in Unit 5.)

Lesson 1—Introduction to Strata

Objective

Students will identify which objects are most recent by looking at a drawing of strata.

Materials

Introduction to Strata worksheet (one per student) • Transparency—Strata • bucket of dirt • tall, clear bottle (2-liter soda bottle with the top cut off works well) • arrowhead • several burnt matchsticks • 5" x 1" piece of fence • button • 1–2" doll • 1" book • several nails • 1" picture of a cow skull • several small sticks • 2" skyscraper (Items may be cut from the Artifacts 1 page, or "real" items/toys may be used.)

Critical Thinking Skill

• Application

Step One: Introducing the Lesson

Gather the materials on a table at the front of the room. Place a small layer of dirt in the bottle. As you read the story below, add the appropriate objects or dirt when you see a *. Place them close to the side of the bottle so that they can still be seen when the next layer of dirt is added.

*A long, long time ago, a young boy sat next to the fire pit in his village to make a new arrowhead from stone. He was nearly finished when a strong earthquake shook the village. As everyone ran, yelling in fear, he dropped the arrowhead. Someone else kicked the fire, and soon the whole village and the forest around it were on fire *(add burnt logs [matches] add arrowhead). The boy and his tribe ran for their lives. They survived the fire by hiding in a cave. The medicine man told them that they could not rebuild their village in the same place.*

Everything of importance to them had burned, so they did not return. Instead, the medicine man led them to a new place.

Each year the wind blew dirt over the fire-torched land. Plants grew and died. After many years, there was no trace of the village. The land was covered by several feet of dirt *(add 1–2 inches of dirt).

Then a young man came with his wife and two little girls in a covered wagon. They built a log cabin. After several years, they decided to go back to the city to live. It was only after they left that the little girl realized she had left her doll and her book. Later, a tornado blew the cabin over. Some of the logs were eaten by bugs and some were taken by passing hikers for firewood, but a few remained *(add doll, book, and logs from cabin). Every year more and more dust was blown over the remnants of the house; plants grew and died there. It took almost a hundred years until the cabin was completely covered with dirt and rock *(add 1–2 inches of dirt).

Then a farmer came to the land and decided it would be a great place to raise cattle. He built a wire fence around the land. One day, he climbed over the fence and tore a button off his shirt. It fell into the grass. He looked for it, but couldn't find it, so he went home. That winter the river flooded, covered the fence with mud, and killed all his cows *(add button, cow skull, and wire fence). The farmer went to find another place to live *(add 1–2 inches of dirt).

Other farmers moved in and plowed the fields, throwing dust over the land. Storms blew dust over the fields in the winter.

Eventually, a road was built over the field. A young girl was riding her bicycle down the road with a bag of tacks. The bike hit a bump and some of the tacks spilled out. She stopped and picked them up, but she did not realize that some of the tacks had rolled into a small crack in the road *(add tacks).

When the road was paved again, the tacks were covered. Twenty years later, a huge skyscraper was built on the spot *(place skyscraper on top).

If you were able to slice through the land we were just talking about, you would see layers, just like you see in this bottle. Archaeologists call these layers "strata."

Ask students to look at the strata and to decide which stratum is the oldest. Explain to students that "stratum" is singular for the word "strata" and that it is used to describe only one layer of strata. Then have students close their eyes. Ask them, *"Who thinks it is the top stratum? Who thinks it is the bottom stratum?"* Most, if not all, will say the bottom stratum is the oldest. Choose several students to tell why they thought the bottom layer was the oldest.

Step Two: Independent Practice

Distribute a copy of the Introduction to Strata page to each student. Depending on the level of the students, this exercise may be done individually or as a group.

Students will draw the given objects in the boxes on the right side of the page. Remind them that boxes D and B must show a layer of dirt, rocks, and other natural debris. On the left side of the page, students will write a short story explaining how the objects ended up in that location. Students should also include a couple of sentences in their narrative about the layers of dirt.

Alternative Lesson

Place the Transparency—Strata page on the overhead projector, covering all but the bottom layer with a sheet of paper. Read the same story as above and uncover one stratum each time you see a *.

Lesson 1—Part II

Objective

Students will write a short fictional story explaining how artifacts and other objects came to be found in a particular location.

Materials

Deeper is Older worksheet and Archaeological Record worksheet (one copy of each for each student) • colored pencils or crayons for each student • classroom clock

Critical Thinking Skill

• Synthesis

Step One: Guided Practice

Distribute Deeper is Older worksheet and drawing materials. Begin with layer 1, which starts at the bottom of the page. Students will record the current time in the Time column next to Start. Then they will color the objects in the Objects column, section 1 only. As they are coloring, they should discuss a possible story to go along with the objects. They will then write one sentence in the Objects box to describe what happened. Explain to students that this activity works best if they take their time and do an excellent job of coloring the objects. Students record their end time once they have finished coloring and writing the sentence for the section.

Move to layer 2. Have students write down the new time in the Time column and repeat steps for objects 2 through 7.

When students are finished with the page, tell them what the finishing time is. Students write this down in the Time column next to End. For each layer, students will subtract the beginning time from the finishing time and record the number of minutes in the Minutes Passed column. (Accuracy is not highly important.) Then they will multiply the minutes passed times 20 to come up with the number of years passed. They write this in the Age in Years column.

Step Two: Independent Practice

Distribute the Archaeological Record worksheet. Working with the Deeper is Older worksheet, students will pretend that they are archaeologists digging in this area. They will choose one object from each stratum on the Deeper is Older worksheet, beginning with the newest stratum at the top of the page (layer 7). On the Archaeological Record worksheet, students will record a description of the object found, its age in years, and a suggestion as to how the object came to be where it was found. Referencing the Deeper is Older worksheet, students will record the depth at which the object was found. Each mark in the depth column represents ten years. The mark at the top of the column represents ten years; the mark at the bottom of the column represents 350 years.

Step Three: Closure

The teacher will choose an object from the Deeper is Older worksheet. Students will write a paragraph on the back of their worksheet describing how the object may have been left behind. Share answers as a class.

OBJECTS	DEPTH	TIME	MINUTES PASSED	X 20	AGE IN YEARS
7 [TEA] A tea party was interrupted by an earthquake.	10	End: 10:35 Start: 10:30	5	X 20	100

Deeper is Older sample entry from page 7

DESCRIPTION OF OBJECT	HOW DID THIS OBJECT END UP THERE?	AGE IN YEARS	DEPTH IN FEET
7 metal horn used to play music	A man played the trumpet in the band. It fell out of his buggy as he drove home one night, and he never found it.	100	15

Archaeological Record sample entry from page 8

Introduction to Strata

Directions: Choose some of the objects below and draw them on the strata (or layers) shown at the right. Then write a story telling how the objects may have come to be in those strata. Boxes B and D must show a layer of dirt, rocks, and other natural debris.

Name _____

Story:

_____

_____

_____

_____

_____

_____

_____

_____

_____

_____

_____

_____

1. Which stratum (singular of strata) is the oldest?

   _____

2. Which stratum is the most recent? _____

3. Which object that you drew is the oldest? _____

4. Which object is the newest? _____

5. If you were going to dig up these strata, which would you find first? _____

   Is this object the oldest or the newest stratum?

   _____

A
B
C
D
E

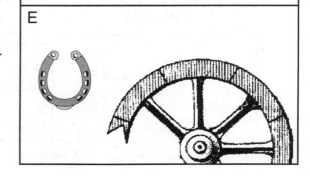

Artifacts 1

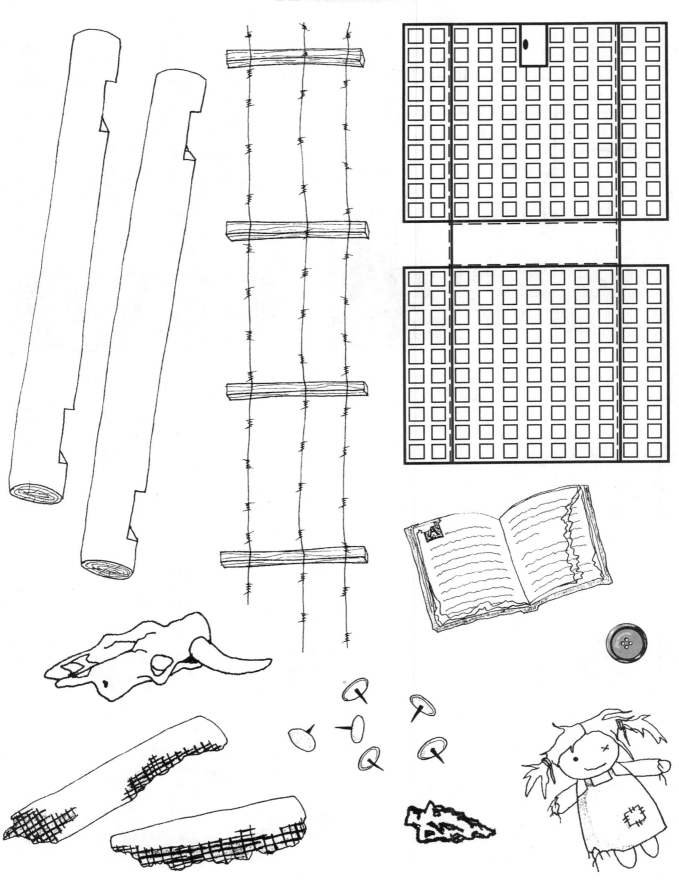

Transparency—Strata

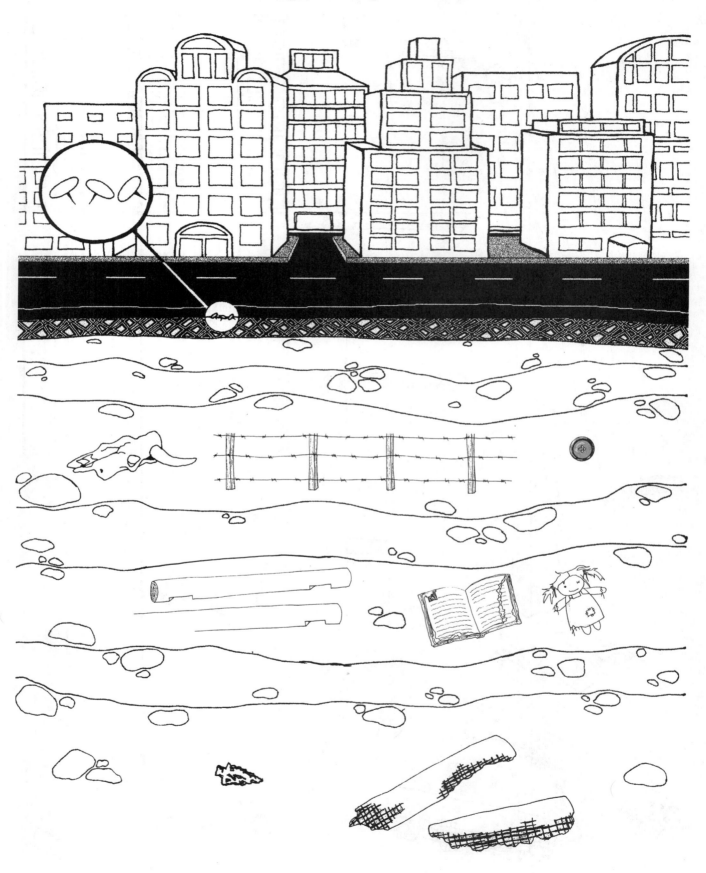

Deeper is Older

Name _____

OBJECTS	DEPTH	TIME	MINUTES PASSED	X 20	AGE IN YEARS
7	10	End: Start:		X 20	
6		End: Start:		X 20	
5		End: Start:		X 20	
4		End: Start:		X 20	
3		End: Start:		X 20	
2		End: Start:		X 20	
1	350	End: Start:		X 20	

Archaeological Record

Name _____

DESCRIPTION OF OBJECT	HOW DID THIS OBJECT END UP THERE?	AGE IN YEARS	DEPTH IN FEET
7			
6			
5			
4			
3			
2			
1			

Chapter 2
Writing the Field Notebook

Background Information

Once archaeologists decide where they are going to excavate, they send a team to survey the area. The survey team draws a contour map that shows all the hills, depressions, rivers, and stream beds in and around the area. An archaeologist then draws a rectangle outlining the dig area. He/she makes sure that the dig is lined up so that two sides lie exactly north and south, and two sides lie exactly east and west. The rectangle is then divided into exact squares. The size of the square depends on how deep they plan to dig. If they plan to dig five feet deep, the squares will probably be 5' x 5'. If they plan to dig ten feet deep, the squares will probably be 10' x 10'. The rectangular grid is labeled with a row number and column letter on its horizontal and vertical axis, respectively. This grid is then transferred to the ground using stakes and string. Each square is carefully dug out one small layer at a time. When an object is located, it is drawn on the grid, or field square horizontal plan, in the correct location. Before the object is removed, it is measured, assigned a serial number, and photographed. Once removed, it is placed in a bag that is labeled with its square number, its serial number, a description, the depth at which it was found, and any significant observations by the archaeologist, including notes about objects found near it. The object is then described completely in a field notebook. Before archaeologists begin excavating the next stratum, all of the dirt and/or objects from the first stratum are removed from each square.

Lesson 1—Field Square Plan Practice

Objective

Students will locate and place objects using a coordinate system on a field square plan.

Materials

Large, flat box (a soda pop flat works well) • dirt • ruler • string • masking tape • 7 small, simple objects • 1/2 page of unlined paper and Field Square

Plan Practice worksheet (one of each for each student)

Critical Thinking Skill

• Application

Step One: Introducing the Lesson

Prepare a classroom dig according to the directions at the end of lesson two in this chapter. Place seven unusual objects in the squares of the dig according to the plan shown below. These will be the artifacts in your dig. Each symbol below represents one artifact. The artifacts may be laid on top of a single layer of dirt to save the time that it takes to excavate them.

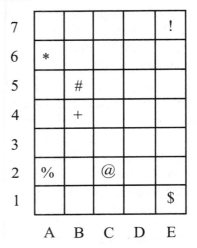

Artifact #	Symbol	Coordinates
1	%	A2
2	!	E7
3	#	B5
4	*	A6
5	$	E1
6	@	C2
7	+	B4

Divide students into small groups. Distribute a half-sheet of paper to each student. Have students fold it in thirds (like a letter) and then unfold it. Ask them to think about the things that they have learned about archaeology. Ask them, *Why don't archaeologists use bulldozers to dig up things from the past?* Write your answer on the blackboard: Archaeologists don't use bulldozers because they might break artifacts. Students copy your answer onto the top section of their paper. In the second section, ask students to come up with their own answers. When students have had enough time to answer, ask them to talk to other people in their group to find a third, different answer. They will write the third answer on the third section of their paper. Discuss answers as a class.

If no one came up with answers related to strata or location, ask these questions: *1. What would happen to the strata if a bulldozer dug through them? 2. What would happen to the objects in the strata? 3. Why would this make an archaeologist's job very difficult? 4. What would happen to the location of artifacts in the dig? 5. How would this make an archaeologist's job more difficult?*

Answers: **1.** If archaeologists used a bulldozer, the strata and the objects in them would get mixed up. **2.** They would not be able to tell which objects were in the upper strata and which objects came from deeper strata. **3.** The archaeologists would not be able to tell which objects were older and which were more recent. They also would not be able to tell which objects came from the same strata and, therefore, from the same time period. **4.** If they used a bulldozer, the original location of the objects would be changed. **5.** Archaeologists would not be able to tell which things had been lying close together.

Step Two: Guided Practice

Teacher Script: *Archaeologists keep records of everything they find in their dig so they can make sure the strata stay in order and so that they can remember where they found each object. Archaeologists divide their digs into squares like graph paper and label the squares. Different teams of diggers are assigned to different squares. They use tools like small trowels, paintbrushes, and wooden picks to slowly remove the dirt, inch by inch and layer by layer. They label everything they find and draw it on a piece of paper that has been divided into squares like the dig. Then they describe the objects in their field notebooks. This is called a field square plan. Today, you are going to practice working with a field square plan just like an archaeologist.*

Show students your classroom dig. Explain that the archaeologists have already divided the dig into squares and dug the dirt from the top stratum. It is now their job to record what was found and where.

Instruct them to look at the Field Square Plan

Practice page. Show them that the letters and numbers on the Plan are similar to the letters and numbers on the site. Point out artifact 1 on the classroom dig to your students and show them how to identify its location by looking at its row number and column letter. Explain that these are its coordinates. Repeat this procedure with artifact 2. One at a time, point out artifacts 3, 4, and 5. Ask students to silently figure out the coordinates of each artifact's location. Then ask for volunteers to offer their answers orally.

Finally, ask students to find the coordinates for artifact 6, and write their answers on question 1 of their Field Square Plan Practice worksheet. Check to make sure all students understand. Show students artifact 7 and ask them to find the coordinates of its location, and write their answer on question 2. Then ask them to complete question 3. Check to make sure all students understand. Ask students to complete question 4.

Step Three: Independent Practice

Students will complete the remainder of the page independently.

Step Four: Closure

Ask students to draw a large red X in C5. Ask them to write the coordinates of the capital letter P in the upper right hand corner of their worksheet. (CLOSURE ANSWER: D2)

Alternative Lesson

Use the Transparency—Field Square Plan page instead of making a dig.

Lesson 2—The Archaeological Dig

Objective

Students will catalog objects from an archaeological dig and record the information on the Field Record and an Enlarged Field Square Plan

Materials

The teacher will need a small clear plastic or glass container containing a single object buried in dirt • plastic spoon • paintbrush • overhead projector • Calipers Page • The Dig Plan • The Artifact Key • Artifacts 2 pages • transparency of Field Record worksheet • enlarged Field Square Plan (Draw the Field Square Plan on butcher paper so that it is the same size as the classroom dig.) • Preparing a Classroom Dig Instructions • Transparency—Field Square Plan (if using the Alternative Lesson)

Each group will need a classroom dig consisting of only one stratum (See Instructions at the end of this lesson) • enlarged Field Square Plan

Each student will need Calipers Page • small paintbrush • plastic spoon • paper plate or bowl • one copy of the Field Record page

Critical Thinking Skill

• Application

Step One: Introducing the Lesson

Teacher Script: *Today, you are going to pretend to be archaeologists on a dig. Real archaeologists spend years digging at one site. We don't have time to do that, so our dig is very small. All the artifacts are small, like models of the real artifacts. The dig you will work on today is an artificial dig. You will work on the dig as a team so that you can learn how an archaeological dig works.*

Distribute the Calipers Page. Students will cut out the caliper parts. Students will assemble the calipers by gluing parts B and C to the corresponding, shaded areas of part A. Be sure to tell students to use only a small amount of glue and to place glue only on the shaded areas of part A. When the glue has set, slide part D in between parts B and C. It should slide back and forth easily. Before the lesson, assemble a sample so students will have an example to look at.

Explain to students that these calipers are like the metal ones used by archaeologists to measure the size of objects they dig up. Using the sample caliper and a rounded object, demonstrate how to measure the object's height and width. Place the object between the "fingers" of the calipers. Read the measurement that is indicated by the arrow on part C.

Step Two: Acquiring Information

Teacher Script: *Your group is your archaeological team, and together you must use all the skills you have learned so far. Each person in your team will be assigned several squares to excavate.*

Archaeologists must take great care when they are digging. They want to make sure they do not miss anything, even if it is small. When you dig, you should take only one-quarter of an inch of dirt off the top of a square at one time. Finish one square before moving on to another. When all of your squares have had one-quarter of an inch removed, then you will start over again, removing another one-quarter of an inch. When you uncover part of an artifact, do not immediately pull it out. Use your spoon to remove most of the dirt, and then use your brush to clean it off.

Use the Field Record sheet to write about the artifact. You will measure the object with your calipers, draw it, write down the coordinates of the square in which it was found, write down what it looks like, and answer the two questions. Then you will tape the object in its correct location on your group's Field Square Plan. (If you are using objects instead of the paper artifacts, the students may lay the objects in their correct location on the Field Square Plan.)

Step Three: Guided Practice

Distribute the Field Record worksheet to each student. Place your small clear plastic or glass container in a central location where all students can see. Begin to excavate the dirt, one-quarter of an inch at a time with the spoon. Put the excavated dirt on a paper plate or bowl. Continue this process until you uncover part of the object. Reiterate to students the importance of leaving the object in place until it has been completely excavated. Excavate the object. Brush off clinging dirt with the paint brush.

Place the Field Record Transparency on the overhead projector. Ask students to record the information about the artifact on their Field Record worksheet as you write the information on the transparency. Choose any coordinates.

Each student writes his/her name as recorder. Measure the length and width of the object with the calipers and record it on the appropriate lines. Write a description of the object. (You can ask for student participation or ask them to complete it on their own.) Draw the object in the drawing box. Ask for volunteers to explain how the object was used and what it tells about the people who used it. Record the answers on the correct lines. Demonstrate the placement of the artifact on the enlarged Field Square Plan.

Step Four: Independent Practice

Divide students into small groups (four is ideal). Distribute the dig and all materials. Assign squares to students. Do not assign a row of squares to a single student, as they will get in each other's way. Assign them so each student has a block of squares. For example, in a group of four students, one student might be assigned to A-1, A-2, A-3, B-1, B-2, B-3, C-1, C-2, and C-3.

Explain to students that they are going to excavate the squares they are assigned, digging exactly as they were just shown. They will record their findings on their Field Record worksheet. Students will attach their artifacts to the enlarged Field Square Plan with tape. Offer incentives to the teams displaying the best archaeological technique. Students will excavate their squares and record their findings on their Field Record worksheet. Each team will report their findings to the class.

Alternative Lesson

Complete Steps 1–3. For Step 4, divide students into small groups. Using the Artifacts 2 pages, make a set of artifacts for each group. Using The Dig Plan as a guide, cut the artifacts apart and write the correct coordinates on the back of each one. Place the artifacts into a large container or manila envelope. Distribute the artifacts to each group along with the enlarged Field Square Plan. Each student in the group will pull out a single artifact from the container or envelope. They will record its information on their Field Record worksheets just as if they had uncovered the artifact in a dig. They will copy the coordinates from the back of the artifact. When they have finished recording the artifact, they will attach the artifact to the enlarged Field Square Plan at its correct coordinates using tape or glue. Then they will pull out a second artifact from the container and repeat the procedure. The members of each team will continue to draw the artifacts until all artifacts have been recorded.

Preparing the Classroom Dig Instructions

Materials

Large shallow box or tray • dirt • spray bottle • string • masking tape • artifacts • large permanent marker • clear contact paper (optional)

Preparation

Locate a flat, shallow box that is at least 5 inches high. Fill it with approximately one inch of dirt. Moisten the dirt with a spray bottle so it is damp. Lay the artifacts on the dirt according to The Dig Plan. Artifacts may need to be folded in order to fit into the squares. Cover with approximately two inches of dirt. Moisten the dirt again.

Pictures of artifacts are provided with the lessons. If these are cut out and covered with clear adhesive paper, they can be used year after year. They may also be supplemented or replaced by objects. Objects should be as similar to the paper ones as possible. On The Dig Plan, you will see a section marked "smooth rocks—no pattern." This section is intended to represent a dry stream bed. You may use pea gravel or aquarium gravel. To form the hardened mud ditch, listed as #18 on The Dig Plan, cut a piece of brown construction paper five inches long and six inches wide. Fold accordion-style into 3/4 inch pleats. Stretch it out to form four "mud ditches."

Using a ruler, make a mark on all four sides of your box in three-inch, four-inch, or five-inch increments. Cut pieces of string the length and width of the box plus two inches. Tape one end of one piece of string to one of the marks. Tape the other end to the mark on the opposite side of the box. Strings should be taut and should rest as close to the dirt as possible. Repeat this process with each set of marks until you have created a grid in the box.

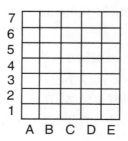

Place pieces of masking tape on the edge of the box between the marks. Use the marker to label the rows 1, 2, 3, etc. and the columns A, B, C, etc. The letters and numbers should be at least one inch high.

Field Square Plan Practice

Name _____

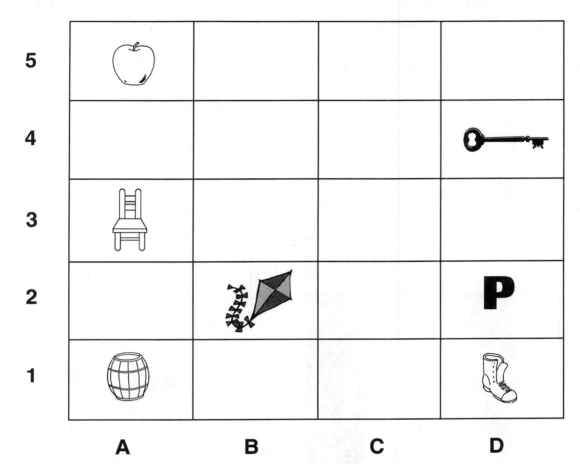

1. Write the coordinates for artifact 6 _____

2. Write the coordinates for artifact 7 _____

3. Draw a in D4.

4. Draw a in A2.

Write the coordinates for each of these objects.

5. _____

7. _____

9.  _____

6. _____

8. _____

10. _____

Draw the following objects in the correct square.

11. **A1**

13. **A** **C5**

15.  **D3**

12. **B4**

14. **A4**

16. **C2**

Calipers Page

Directions: Glue parts B and C to the corresponding, shaded areas of part A. Place a small amount of glue on the shaded areas of part A. When the glue has set, slide part D in between parts B and C. It should slide back and forth easily.

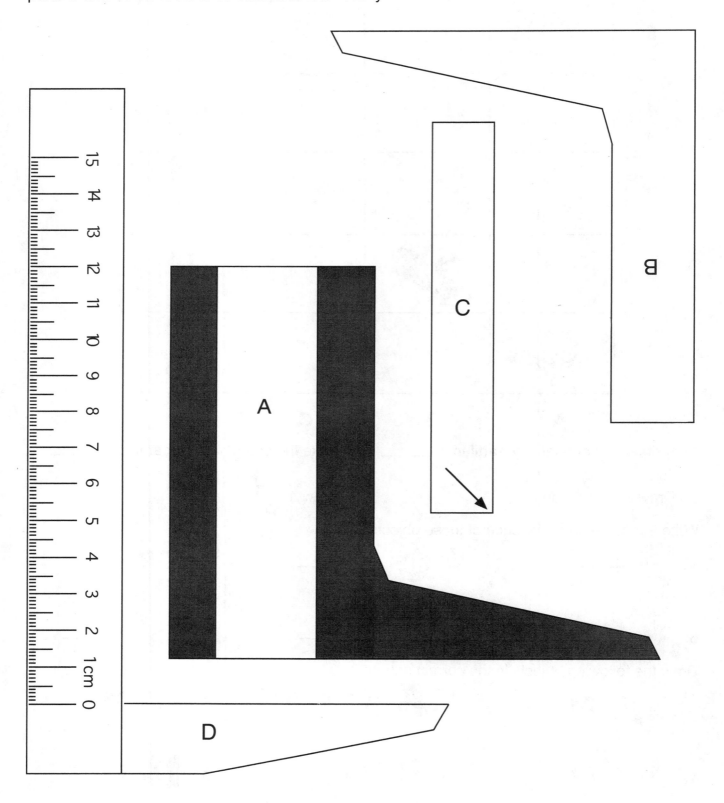

The Dig Plan

Directions: The circled numbers below represent where the artifacts on the Artifacts 2 pages should go in your classroom digs.

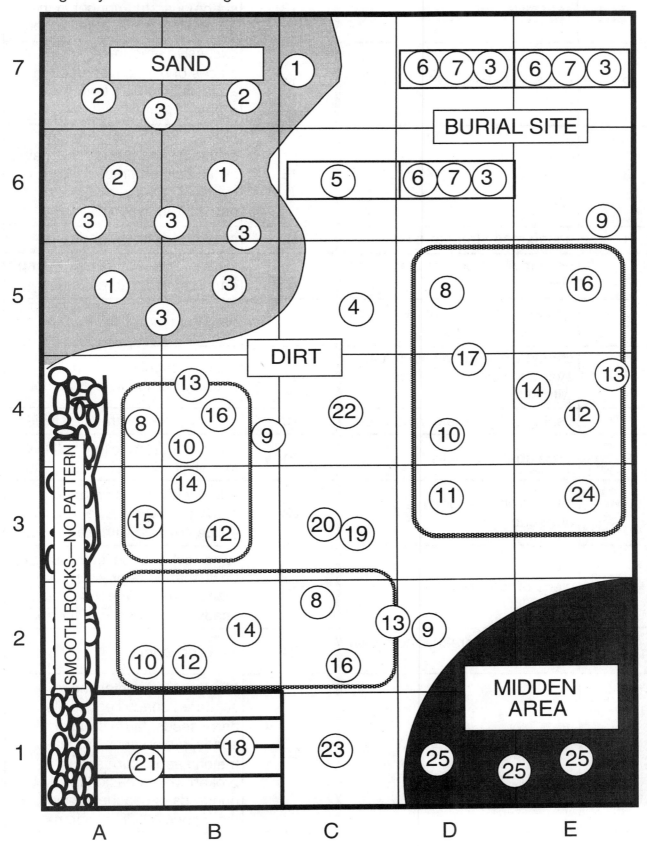

The Artifact Key

1	seashells	13	broken wooden poles (round in shape) inserted upright in the ground in a rectangular shape
2	dolphin skeleton	14	excessive amount of large pieces of bark covering other artifacts inside rectangular areas
3	seaweed	15	basket containing ten small sticks painted black, ten small sticks painted green, and twenty small sea creatures carved from wood
4	canoe made from tree bark	16	strings of copper beads
5	dolphin skeleton wrapped in red cloth	17	cloth scrolls with picture writing on them, tied with red string
6	human skeleton wrapped in red cloth, feet facing the sea	18	hardened mud ditch
7	carved wooden dolphin mask over each skeleton, covered with kelp	19	rocks in circular pattern, partially burned logs in center
8	fishing nets made of nylon cord	20	grass baskets with rocks inside
9	large abalone shells	21	hoe made from a seashell tied to a stick
10	tan, brown, and green spindles of thread	22	3-foot-wide domed structure made of river clay, very hard, inside covered with black soot
11	piece of red cloth	23	large rock with several rounded bowl-shaped depressions on the top, some wheat flour and seeds in the cracks of the rock
12	pieces of tan, green, and brown cloth	24	weaving loom
		25	Midden Area containing scattered seagull eggshells, berry seeds, large squash seeds, melon rinds, large melon seeds, corn seeds, broken woven baskets, hundreds of seashells, and thousands of fish skeletons

Artifacts 2

Directions: Make one copy for each dig. Cut out numbered artifacts and place in the dig according to The Dig Plan on page 15.

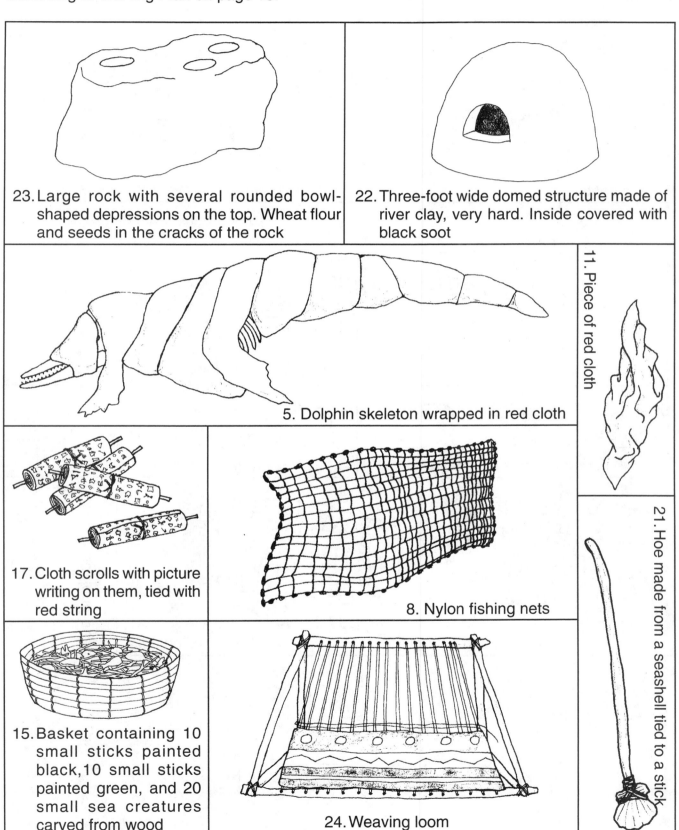

23. Large rock with several rounded bowl-shaped depressions on the top. Wheat flour and seeds in the cracks of the rock

22. Three-foot wide domed structure made of river clay, very hard. Inside covered with black soot

11. Piece of red cloth

5. Dolphin skeleton wrapped in red cloth

17. Cloth scrolls with picture writing on them, tied with red string

8. Nylon fishing nets

21. Hoe made from a seashell tied to a stick

15. Basket containing 10 small sticks painted black,10 small sticks painted green, and 20 small sea creatures carved from wood

24. Weaving loom

Artifacts 2 cont.

Directions: Make one copy for each dig. Cut out numbered artifacts and place in the dig according to The Dig Plan on page 15.

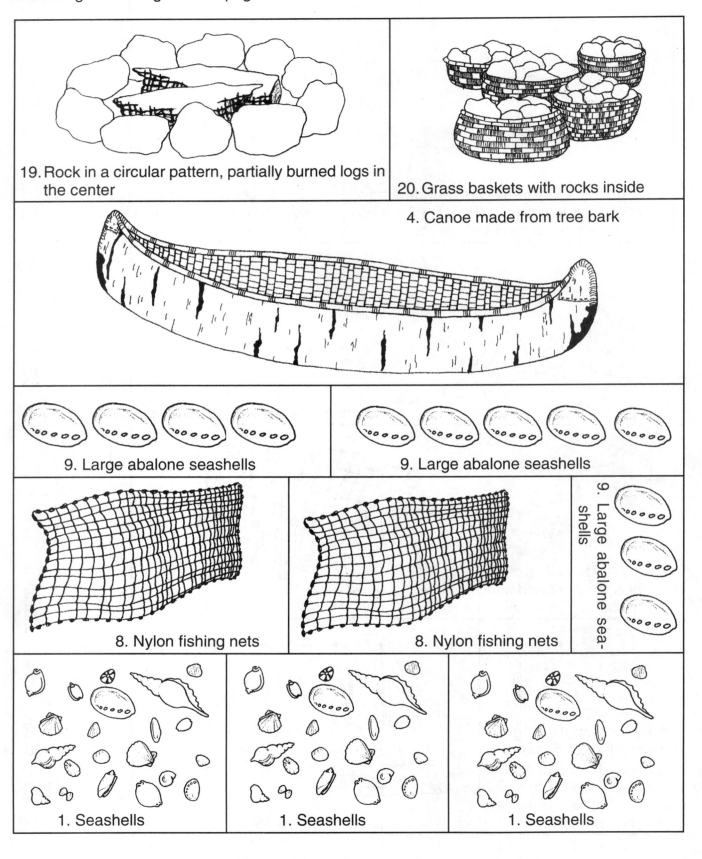

19. Rock in a circular pattern, partially burned logs in the center

20. Grass baskets with rocks inside

4. Canoe made from tree bark

9. Large abalone seashells

9. Large abalone seashells

8. Nylon fishing nets

8. Nylon fishing nets

9. Large abalone sea-shells

1. Seashells

1. Seashells

1. Seashells

Artifacts 2 cont.

Directions: Make three copies for each dig. Cut out numbered artifacts and place in the dig according to The Dig Plan on page 15.

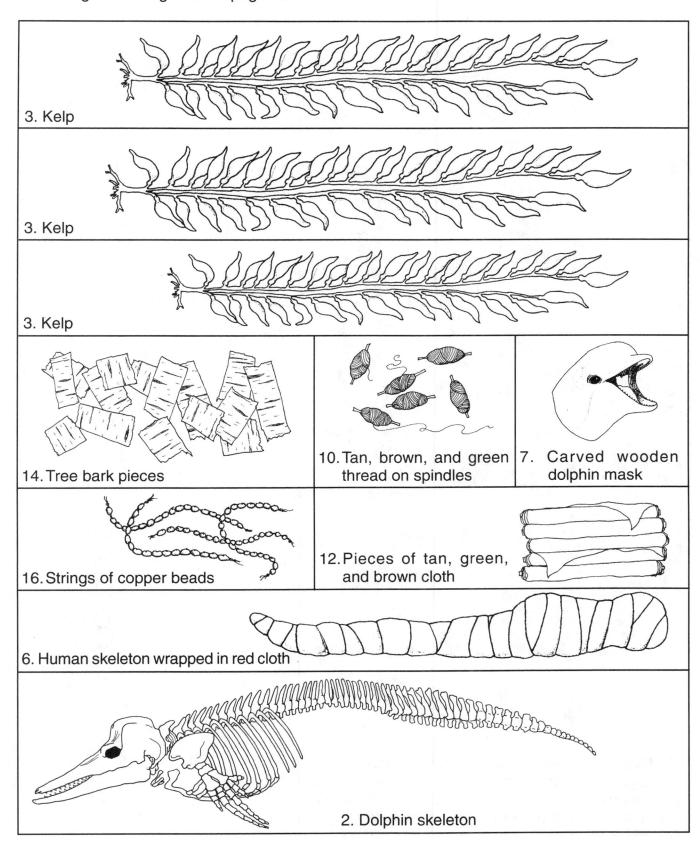

3. Kelp

3. Kelp

3. Kelp

14. Tree bark pieces

10. Tan, brown, and green thread on spindles

7. Carved wooden dolphin mask

16. Strings of copper beads

12. Pieces of tan, green, and brown cloth

6. Human skeleton wrapped in red cloth

2. Dolphin skeleton

Artifacts 2 cont.

Directions: Make three copies for each dig. Cut out numbered artifacts and place in the dig according to The Dig Plan on page 15.

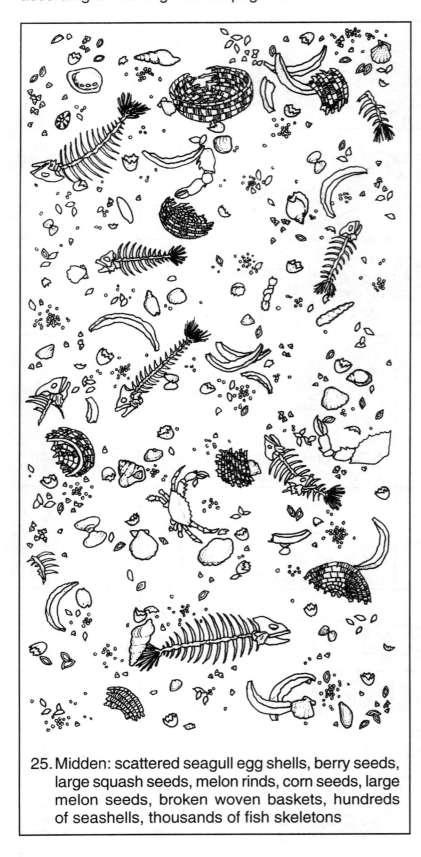

13. Broken wooden poles inserted upright in the ground. (Cut out poles in strips.)

25. Midden: scattered seagull egg shells, berry seeds, large squash seeds, melon rinds, corn seeds, large melon seeds, broken woven baskets, hundreds of seashells, thousands of fish skeletons

Field Record

Date _____   Location Coordinates _____   Recorder _____
Length _____ Width _____
Full Description _____
_____
_____
How was it used? _____
What does it tell you about these people? _____
_____

Date _____   Location Coordinates _____   Recorder _____
Length _____ Width _____
Full Description _____
_____
_____
How was it used? _____
What does it tell you about these people? _____
_____

Date _____   Location Coordinates _____   Recorder _____
Length _____ Width _____
Full Description _____
_____
_____
How was it used? _____
What does it tell you about these people? _____
_____

Date _____   Location Coordinates _____   Recorder _____
Length _____ Width _____
Full Description _____
_____
_____
How was it used? _____
What does it tell you about these people? _____
_____

Date _____   Location Coordinates _____   Recorder _____
Length _____ Width _____
Full Description _____
_____
_____
How was it used? _____
What does it tell you about these people? _____
_____

Field Square Plan

Completed by: _____

	A	B	C	D	E
7					
6					
5					
4					
3					
2					
1					

Transparency—Field Square Plan

UNIT 2
INTERPRETING THE ARTIFACTS

Chapter 1
Location, Location, Location!

Background Information

Archaeologists dig artifacts and other objects from the ground one at a time. Each artifact is important, but it provides only part of the information that the archaeologist seeks. Archaeologists want to know about the life-styles of the people they are studying. Often there is very little written information about a group of people. Archaeologists must use common sense to put together clues that lead to the truth. Sometimes they uncover an artifact so unusual, they do not know what it is used for.

One of the clues that archaeologists study is the location of the artifacts in relationship to other artifacts. The use or significance of an artifact may be determined by where it was found and what was found near it. For instance, an archaeologist may dig up a small pottery bowl with dark stains inside. There are many possible uses for such a bowl, but the archaeologist wants to find out how this particular bowl was used. As he excavates the area around the bowl, he finds that the bowl was sitting on the ground next to a stone altar. He may then make a hypothesis that the bowl was used in some kind of religious ritual. On the other hand, if the archaeologist digs around the bowl and finds many different kinds of roots and herbs that have medicinal qualities, he may then make the hypothesis that the bowl was used to mix medicines. Perhaps the bowl is found near a well. Then the archaeologist may make the hypothesis that water was drunk from the bowl. If the bowl was one of a set that was found in a house, he may make the hypothesis that it was an individual food container.

In the following lessons, students will again be asked to act as archaeologists. They will be asked to look at artifacts and make hypotheses as to what the items may have been used for. There are no wrong answers as long as students can justify their answers.

Lesson 1—Location and Use

Objective

Students will form a theory about the use and significance of an object or artifact from its proximity to other objects or artifacts.

Materials

Location, Location, Location! Part I and Location, Location, Location! Part II worksheets (one of each per student) • Dried baby's breath or herbs on stems • pipe (real one, paper one, or one made from a cork and a piece of drinking straw) • wooden beam (pictures of artifacts on the Artifacts 3 page may be used instead of the real items)

Critical Thinking Skills

- Inductive Reasoning
- Hypothesizing
- Evaluation

Step One: Introducing the Lesson

Show students a bunch of dried vegetation. Tell them that it was dug up in an archaeological dig. Ask them to suggest what these plants might have been used for. Record their answers on the chalkboard or overhead projector.

Hang the plants upside down as if they were hanging from the wooden beam. Ask students how they think the plants might have been used if they had found them hanging from a roof rafter near a fireplace. *(They used them as spices for cooking.)* Ask students how they came to their answer. *(Cooks would want spices close to their cooking place. [Perhaps students have seen spices hanging from rafters in old pictures.])* Ask students which artifacts gave them clues about how the plants were used *(rafter, fireplace).*

Hold up the plants and the pipe. Suggest that the plants had been found next to the pipe. Ask them how they think the plants might have been used. *(They were smoked in the pipe.)* Ask students which artifacts gave them clues about how the plants were used *(pipe)*.

Place the plants in the manger. Suggest that the plants had been found in a barn in a manger. Ask them how they think the plants might have been used. *(They were used to feed farm animals.)* Ask students which artifacts gave them clues about how the plants were used *(manger, barn)*.

Point out to students that archaeologists would have a difficult time figuring out how an object was used if they didn't know what objects were found nearby. An archaeologist cannot figure out how people in ancient times lived without carefully looking at the location of all the objects he digs up.

Step Two: Guided Practice

Distribute Location, Location, Location! Part I worksheet. Ask students to look at pictures A and B. Each of these boxes represent strata that have been excavated from different digs in different places in the world. Divide students into small groups and ask them to discuss the importance of the location of the artifacts. Students should work together to answer the questions.

Share and discuss students' answers. If time permits, ask students to suggest any ideas they might have about the habits of these people based on the pictures.

Step Three: More Guided Practice

Ask students to look at pictures C and D. Each of these boxes are strata that have been excavated from different digs in different places in the world. Ask students to work individually this time. They should make every effort to answer the questions with a minimum of assistance from the teacher.

Share and discuss students' answers. If time permits, teachers may ask students to suggest any ideas they might have about the habits of these people based on the pictures.

Step Four: Independent Practice

Distribute Location, Location, Location! Part II worksheet. Students will complete the worksheet independently.

Location, Location, Location! Part I

Name _____

A

1. How did the people use the couch in picture A? _____
_____

2. What artifacts gave clues to help you?
_____
_____

3. What does the couch's location tell you about the people who used it? _____
_____

B

1. How did the people use the couch in picture B? _____
_____

2. What artifacts gave clues to help you?
_____
_____

3. What does the picture tell you about the people who used it? _____
_____

C

1. How did the people use the rope in picture C? _____

2. What artifacts gave clues to help you?
_____
_____

3. What does the rope's location tell you about the people who used it? _____
_____

D

1. How did the people use the rope in picture D? _____

2. What artifacts gave clues to help you?
_____
_____

3. What does the rope's location tell you about the people who used it? _____

Location, Location, Location! Part II

Name _____

A

1. How was the statue in picture A used?
   _____
   _____

2. What objects and artifacts gave clues to help
   you?_____
   _____

3. What does the picture tell you about the
   people who used it? _____
   _____

B

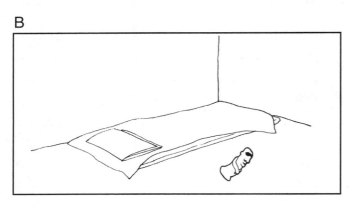

1. How did the people use the statue in
   picture B? _____

2. What artifacts gave clues to help you?
   _____
   _____

3. What does the picture tell you about the
   people who used it? _____
   _____

C

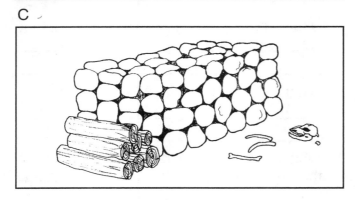

1. How were the rocks in picture C used?
   _____
   _____

2. What artifacts gave clues to help you?
   _____
   _____

3. What does the picture tell you about the
   people who used it? _____
   _____

D

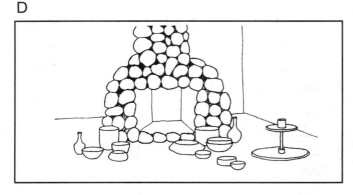

1. How were the rocks in picture D used?
   _____
   _____

2. What artifacts gave clues to help you?
   _____
   _____

3. What does the picture tell you about the
   people who used it? _____
   _____

Artifacts 3

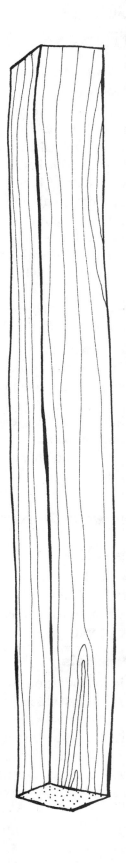

Chapter 2
What Did They Eat?

Background Information

It is important to determine what people of ancient cultures ate because it gives us insight into their life-styles. By looking at what they ate, an archaeologist can make some assumptions as to what tools they may have had, how many people lived together, what kinds of houses they built, how far they traveled from home, and the amount of contact they had with other cultures. For example, if they find evidence of foods not grown or found locally, they may be able to determine which people they traded with. By looking at what people ate, archaeologists can also determine whether the society was a nomadic society of hunter-gatherers, a sedentary agrarian society, or an industrial society.

Garbage piles, or middens, are important sources of information to archaeologists. There they can find bones, skins, vegetable rinds, seeds, broken pots, and discarded tools. By looking through the layers of the midden, they can even chart dietary changes in a group of people over time. Changes in diet may help shed light on changes in living conditions and life-style.

Lesson 1—Middens

Objective

Students will examine food remains from a simulated archaeological dig and make reasonable suggestions as to the diet, life-style, and eating habits of the people.

Materials

Midden Questions worksheet (three copies for each student) • Midden Practice Part I and Midden Practice Part II worksheets (one copy for each student) • miscellaneous garbage (suggested garbage: 5 candy bar wrappers, 7 frozen vegetable bags or empty vegetable cans, ice cream carton, meat trays with labels attached, pits or seeds from a variety of fruits and vegetables [make a key to help students identify the types of seeds], empty cereal box, bread wrapper, several milk cartons, orange juice can, cheese wrapper, empty flour and sugar bags, broken wooden or plastic mixing spoon, broken toaster or other cooking appliance • 4 items taken from the midden in the Classroom Dig

Critical Thinking Skills

• Synthesis

• Analysis

Step One: Introducing the Lesson

Bring in a garbage can or garbage bag full of garbage. (If the garbage is clean, it can be stored and used from year to year.)

Teacher Script: *I want you to think back to the stories that I told you when we were first beginning to learn about strata. I told these stories while I filled the bottle with dirt. The first story I told was about the boy who was making arrowheads when his village caught fire after the earthquake. If archaeologists were to dig up the boy's village, would they find houses in good condition with cooking tools and beds in their original place?* (No.) *Why not?* (It was all burned.) *What might an archaeologist find?* (Answers vary—maybe some partly burned houses or clothes. Some tools made from stone or bone might be found. The boy's arrowhead or the stones around the fire pit may still be there.) *It is unusual for an archaeologist to find an entire house or village completely intact with everything still in it. Archaeologists spend most of their time studying things that have been left behind. But there is something that is left behind in almost every village or town that is a treasure for archaeologists—garbage dumps. Archaeologists call them "middens."*

When archaeologists look at people's garbage, they can begin to understand not only what they ate, but how they lived. If they find cans and boxes made in a factory, they know that the people knew how to make complex machinery. If they find only clothing sewn by hand, they can assume that people made their own clothing and that they did not have sewing machines. By studying middens, archaeologists can tell how people travelled and how they lived. They can tell whether the people were farmers or if they had factories. If they find things that cannot be found locally, then they know that the people must have traded with others to get them.

Sometimes what is not found is as important as what is found. For instance, if deer are common in the area and there is no evidence that deer were eaten, an archaeologist must ask why. By looking at the other artifacts and objects, the archaeologist may decide that there were religious reasons that the deer were not eaten. Perhaps these people considered the deer a sacred animal. Or maybe the archaeologist figures out that the people did not know how to make the tools to hunt the deer.

Today, we are going to look at some middens the way an archaeologist would. We are going to see what we can learn about people by looking at their garbage.

Step Two: Guided Practice

Distribute the Midden Questions worksheet. Remove the garbage from the container and set the contents where students can view it. Work through the questions on the worksheet with students, discussing their ideas.

Step Three: More Guided Practice

Divide students into groups of four. Distribute one copy of the Midden Practice Part I page to each group and a second copy of the Midden Questions worksheet to each student. Ask students to work together to complete the Midden Questions worksheet while looking at the Midden Practice Part I page. As a class, compare students' answers to the Midden Questions worksheet.

Step Four: Independent Practice

Distribute a third copy of the Midden Questions worksheet and a copy of the Midden Practice Part II worksheet to each student. Students should be able to look at the information provided on the Midden Practice Part II worksheet and complete the Midden Questions worksheet independently.

Step Five: Closure

Show students four objects taken from the midden in their archaeological dig. Ask students to list four things that they learned about that society from those objects. Students will write their answers on the back of the Midden Questions worksheet. Ask for volunteers to share their answers. The teacher may want to list the items on the board.

Midden Questions

Name _____

A.

1. What kind of food did these people eat? (Be specific.)

   _____

   _____

2. Were most of them farmers? _____

3. How can you tell? _____

   _____

   _____

4. Were only some of them farmers in their society? _____

5. How can you tell? _____

   _____

   _____

6. Who prepared their food? _____

7. How can you tell? _____

   _____

   _____

B.

List each item and tell one thing that you can learn about the society from that item.

1. _____
2. _____
3. _____
4. _____
5. _____
6. _____
7. _____
8. _____
9. _____
10. _____

Midden Practice Part I

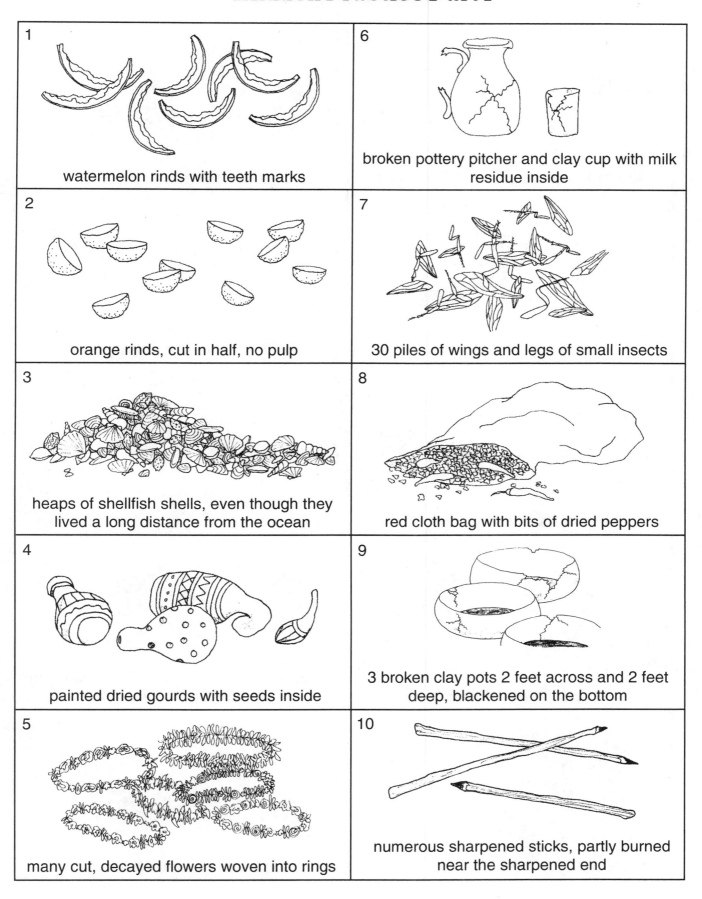

1 watermelon rinds with teeth marks

2 orange rinds, cut in half, no pulp

3 heaps of shellfish shells, even though they lived a long distance from the ocean

4 painted dried gourds with seeds inside

5 many cut, decayed flowers woven into rings

6 broken pottery pitcher and clay cup with milk residue inside

7 30 piles of wings and legs of small insects

8 red cloth bag with bits of dried peppers

9 3 broken clay pots 2 feet across and 2 feet deep, blackened on the bottom

10 numerous sharpened sticks, partly burned near the sharpened end

Midden Practice Part II

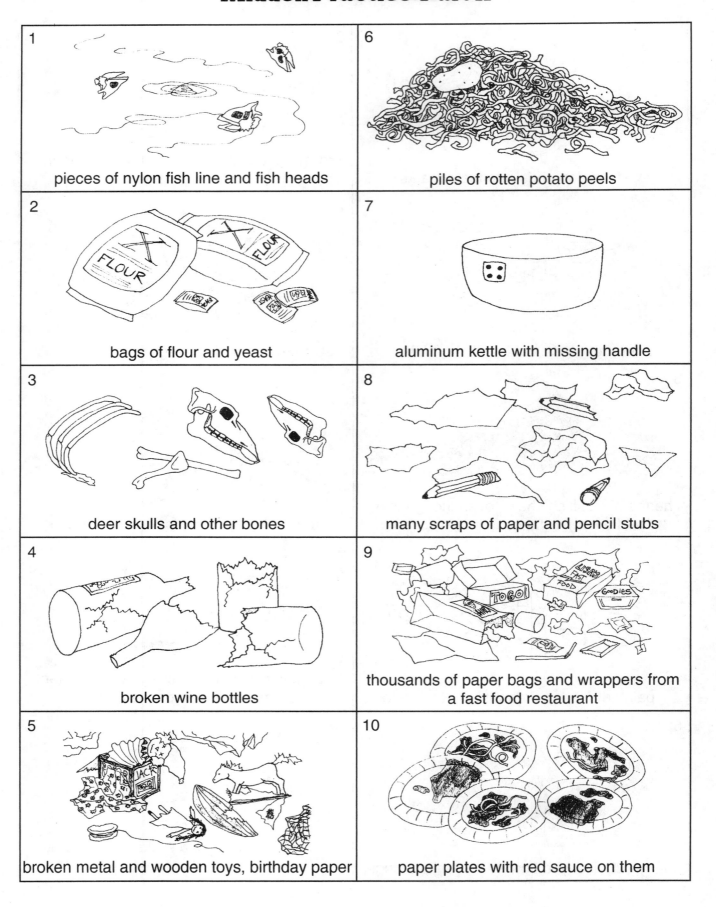

1 pieces of nylon fish line and fish heads

2 bags of flour and yeast

3 deer skulls and other bones

4 broken wine bottles

5 broken metal and wooden toys, birthday paper

6 piles of rotten potato peels

7 aluminum kettle with missing handle

8 many scraps of paper and pencil stubs

9 thousands of paper bags and wrappers from a fast food restaurant

10 paper plates with red sauce on them

Chapter 3
Messages From the Dead

Background

Burial sites are important sources of information about a civilization. They reveal a culture's attitude toward death, which in turn reflects on its attitude toward life. What people believe will happen to them after they die has a direct influence on things they do while they are alive. For example, if a person believes that death is merely the passage to a new and wonderful existence, he/she will not fear death.

Everything that is found in a burial site is potentially significant and needs to be meticulously noted. What were the positions of the bodies? Were all the heads facing east or west? Were the bodies on their knees? Were the hands folded over the chest? The placement of the bodies in relationship to each other may also be significant. Were families buried together? Were men buried in one area and women in another? The items buried with the body usually fall into two categories: things that were important to the person while he/she was alive and things that were considered necessary to the person after his/her death. Some items fall into both categories.

By examining a skeleton, an osteologist (one who studies bones) can determine, with a high degree of accuracy, the age of the person at the time of death, the gender, the approximate height, and often, the cause of death. The skeleton may also provide information about the person's diet, occupation, past accidents, diseases suffered, and the number of children birthed.

Although this information is interesting on an individual basis, the archaeologist studies trends in an entire group of people to build a complete picture of the civilization.

It is not important that students at this level remember any of the details that they work with. For example, it is not important for them to memorize the formula for figuring out the height of a person or to memorize how to figure the age at death from a skeleton. They need to remember only that archaeologists learn about civilizations by studying burial sites.

Lesson 1—Burial Sites

Objective

Students will hypothesize about the attitudes and beliefs of a group of people regarding life and death by studying an archaeologist's report of a burial site.

Materials

Small piece of scratch paper for each student • Burial Sites Part I worksheet and Burial Sites Part II worksheet (one of each for each student)

Critical Thinking Skills

- Synthesis
- Analysis
- Hypothesizing

Step One: Introducing the Lesson

Distribute scratch paper. Ask students to sketch a burial scene. Give students a few minutes to complete their sketches. Ask students to tell what they drew. Record the answers in simple form on the chalkboard—for example, flowers, casket, candles, black clothes, favorite clothes, gravestone, cemetery, cross, rosary beads. Ask students to tell what these things tell about our beliefs about death. For example, we send flowers as a symbol of love and renewal. We preserve the dead bodies as a show of respect. Black clothes indicate sorrow and sadness. We preserve and mark the location of burial so we can return to honor them, speak to them, and pray over them.

Step Two: Guided Practice

Divide students into pairs. Distribute Burial Sites Part I worksheet to each student. Working together, students discuss the society's beliefs about death. Discuss students' answers as a class.

Step Three: Independent Practice

Distribute Burial Sites Part II worksheet to each student. Students will complete this worksheet independently.

Step Four: Closure

Ask students to remember details about the burial site in their archaeological dig. Review details orally with students' assistance. If desired, record the details on the chalkboard. Ask students to write down three things that the people of that culture believe about death. Share their answers with the class. Ask each student to explain to the class how he/she arrived at his/her conclusions.

CLOSURE (Possible Answers):

1. They believed that they became dolphins upon their death.

2. They believed that red was a sacred color.

3. They believed that they needed kelp to eat in their next life.

4. They worshipped dolphins.

5. They believed that a dolphin would lead them to their new life.

6. They believed that they needed to hide the fact that they were human to fool the dolphins.

Lesson 2—Reading the Bones

Objective

Students will tell the gender, height, and age at the time of death by looking at the skeletal remains of a human.

Materials

Each student will receive The Bones Dictionary page • Reading the Bones Part I worksheet • Reading the Bones Part II worksheet • ruler

Critical Thinking Skills

• Synthesis

• Analysis

Step One: Introducing the Lesson

Distribute the Reading the Bones Part I worksheet. Direct students to look at skeleton B. Ask, *What do you know about the living person this skeleton used to be by looking at the bones?* (Students probably won't have very many answers.)

Teacher Script: *When we look at this picture, we see a picture of a skeleton. When archaeologists look*

at this skeleton, they see an open book, full of information about what this person was like when he/she was alive. They can tell how old the person was when he/she died. They can tell whether it was a man or a woman. They can tell how tall the person was. Today, you are going to learn how to read a skeleton just like an archaeologist.

Step Two: Guided Practice

Distribute The Bones Dictionary page on gender. Read the information paragraph with students. Point out the differences between the male and female bones. Then ask students to look at skeleton B on their Reading the Bones Part I worksheet and figure out whether it is male or female. Students will write the answer on line 1. Check students' answers.

Proceed to the section on height. Read the information paragraph on height with students. Show students where the femur bone is located on the skeleton (upper leg). Explain how to use the formula based on femur length to find the skeleton's height. Ask students to compute the height of skeleton B on the Reading the Bones Part I worksheet. Students will write the answer on line 2.

Read the paragraph on age from The Bones Dictionary with students. Ask students to point to the arrows on skeleton A, starting with the youngest bones and moving through to the oldest. Then ask them to look at the arrows on skeleton B from the Reading the Bones Part I worksheet. Ask them to match up the arrows on Skeleton B with the arrows on Skeleton A to find out the age of Skeleton B's bones. When they have found the oldest age, they have found the approximate age at the time of death. Students will write the answer on line 3.

Group students into pairs. They will use The Bones Dictionary page to answer questions about the skeleton at the bottom of the Reading the Bones Part I worksheet.

Step Three: Independent Practice

Distribute the Reading the Bones Part II worksheet. Students will work independently using The Bones Dictionary pages to answer the questions.

Burial Sites Part I

Name _____

Archaeologist's Report

There were twenty-seven bodies buried in this location. Each female skeleton over twelve years old held a candle in one hand and a magnificently painted clay jar in the other. Each clay jar contained valuables such as sapphires, rubies, gold coins, and diamonds. The jars were painted blue with star patterns painted in white. The North Star could be found near the neck of the jar. It was painted much larger than normal with a red circle around it.

In some cases, the hand of a small child's skeleton was holding the hand of the female buried next to it. Around the bodies were the remains of white and brilliant blue silk robes. The men were always buried to the south of the women's bodies. They were placed in a kneeling position so that they faced the women. Many times one of the men's hands was in an outstretched position so that it touched the foot of the nearest woman. The women were always positioned so that their heads were toward the position of the North Star.

1. Why do you think each skeleton held a candle? _____
_____

2. What were the purposes of the clay jar? _____
_____

3. Do these people believe in an afterlife? _____
_____

4. Where do they believe people go when they die? _____
_____

5. What does the child's hand holding the woman's mean? _____
_____

6. Why were the women facing the North Star? _____
_____

7. Why were the men positioned as they were? _____
_____

8. Why were the hands of many of the men touching the foot of a woman? _____
_____

9. Why did the female children under twelve hold no candle or jar of valuables? _____
_____

Burial Sites Part II

Name _____

Archaeologist's Report

This burial site is located deep inside a cave. Just inside the opening of the cave, there was a five-foot deep pit with sharp stakes lining the bottom. There were fifteen bodies at this site. These bodies were laid in long, narrow niches carved from the solid rock. These niches were located at least seven feet above the floor of the cave. The bodies were laid on their sides with the faces facing the interior of the cave and their backs wedged against the solid rock.

All of the faces were covered with hideous masks carved from wood and painted in strange colors. All the eyes painted on the masks were three or four times normal size. Every body, male and female, adult and child, held a weapon of some kind in its hand. There were stone knives and some spears.

The female bodies were found on one side of the cave, and male bodies were found on the other side.

In the middle of the cave, there were two large drums and several finely polished sticks. There were also three hollow reeds with four holes in them. They looked like flutes.

1. Why was a pit placed inside the cave? _____
   _____

2. Why were the bodies inside the cave? _____
   _____

3. Why were the faces of the skeletons covered with masks? _____
   _____

4. Why were the eyes of the masks so large? _____
   _____

5. Why did the skeletons have weapons? _____
   _____

6. Did these people believe in an afterlife? _____
   _____

7. Where did these people believe they went after they died? _____
   _____

8. Why were the bodies facing toward the cave? _____
   _____

9. Why were the females placed on one side of the cave and the males on the other? _____
   _____

10. What were the musical instruments used for? _____
   _____

The Bones Dictionary

GENDER

Archaeologists can tell the difference between male and female skeletons by looking at their skulls and their pelvic (or hip) bones. Female skulls are usually smaller. The jaw is more pointed and the nose opening is more rounded. When a person looks at a male pelvic bone from the top, the opening is narrow and almost heart-shaped. The female pelvic bone has a rounder opening.

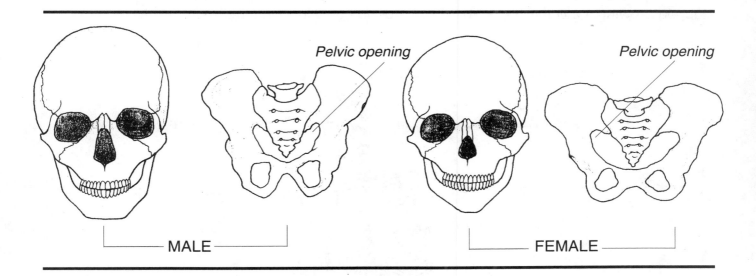

Pelvic opening   *Pelvic opening*

MALE   FEMALE

HEIGHT—MALE

Multiply the length of the femur bone (the long bone in the leg) in inches by 1.88. Then add 32.01 inches to the total. The answer will tell you how tall the man was when he was alive.

Example: The femur bone measured 20.3 inches.

$20.3 \times 1.88 = 38.164$ inches

Then add 32.01: $38.164 + 32.01 = 70.174$ inches

If you divide this number by 12, you will find that this man was slightly more than five feet, ten inches tall.

HEIGHT—FEMALE

Multiply the length of the femur bone (the long bone in the leg) in inches by 1.945. Then add 28.679 inches to the total. The answer will tell you how tall the woman was when she was alive.

*Scientists have similar formulas for other bones in the body.

The Bones Dictionary, cont.

AGE

Most human bones grow from the time a person is a baby until he/she is a teenager. The bones grow at the ends. Different bones reach this point at different ages. By looking at different bones in the body and finding out which ones have stopped growing, the age of a person at the time of death can be determined.

The arrows below show the approximate ages at which some of the bones on this skeleton stopped growing. Only the bones that have stopped growing are labelled.

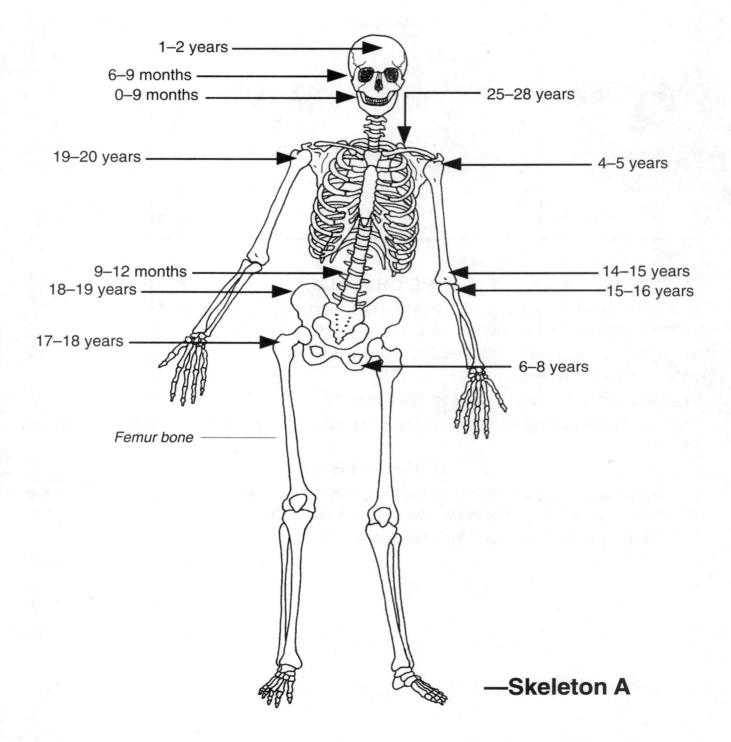

1–2 years

6–9 months

0–9 months

25–28 years

19–20 years

4–5 years

9–12 months

14–15 years

18–19 years

15–16 years

17–18 years

6–8 years

Femur bone

—Skeleton A

© 1999 Critical Thinking Books & Software • www.criticalthinking.com • (800)458-4849

Reading the Bones Part I

Name _____

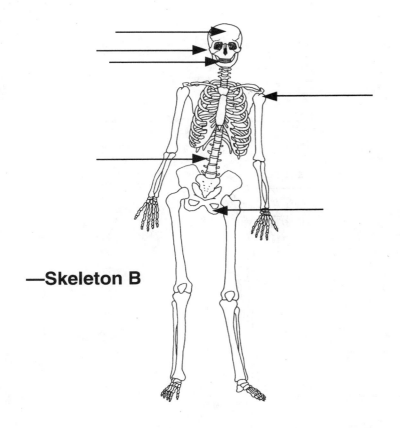

Sex

1. _____

Height

2. _____

Age at time of death

3. _____

SCALE: 2 mm = 1 inch

—Skeleton B

1. Was this person male or femal

   _____

2. How tall was this person?

   _____

3. How old was this person when he/she died?

   _____

SCALE: 2 mm = 1 inch

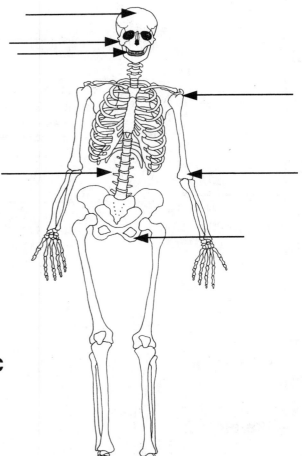

—Skeleton C

Reading the Bones Part II

Name _____

1. Was the person male or female?

   _____

2. How did you know?

   _____

3. How tall was this person?

   _____

4. How old was this person when he/she died?

   _____

5. How did you figure that out?

   _____

SCALE: 2mm = 1 inch

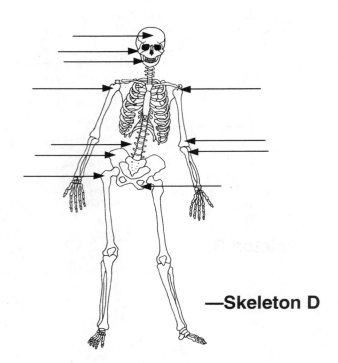

—Skeleton D

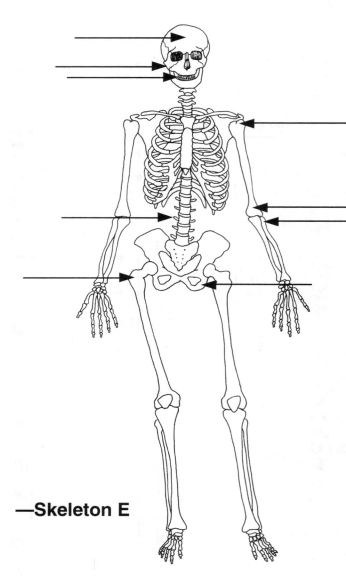

—Skeleton E

1. Was the person male or female?

   _____

2. How did you know?

   _____

3. How tall was this person?

   _____

4. How old was this person when he/she died?

   _____

5. How did you figure that out?

   _____

SCALE: 2mm = 1 inch

UNIT 3
A LOOK AT CULTURE

Chapter 1
A Look at Culture

Background Information

Culture is the way we describe the life-style of a group of people. Culture includes the beliefs, customs, art, achievements, and attitudes that are passed on from generation to generation. The culture of a people is defined by the clothing they wear, the foods they eat, and the houses in which they live.

Culture includes the way people spend their leisure time, the types of sports they play, and the games they create. Culture is reflected in the way people choose to express themselves. The style of artwork and the subjects of paintings and sculptures reveal how people think and feel. Culture is reflected in the style and content of literature. The topics people considered important enough to write about give insight into their everyday lives. Archaeologists are interested in what they laughed about or considered tragic.

From artifacts, archaeologists learn how people made their living and at which skills they excelled. Inventions tell archaeologists how people lived. For example, a Chinese rice farmer would probably not invent an arrow for hunting buffalo.

Culture is affected by the geography and climate people live in. Geography and climate influence the extent to which people travel. How people travel from one place to another is part of their culture.

All of these things are clues to a society's culture, and it is an archaeologist's job to draw conclusions about them.

It is important to remember that only rarely do entire towns or even single houses become preserved, whole and undamaged, with all the contents intact. Most of the artifacts that archaeologists find are things that were abandoned in old houses or warehouses or things that were found in garbage dumps.

Pompeii in Italy is a notable exception. On a summer day in 79 A.D., the sudden eruption of a volcano covered the city in hot, wet ash and poisonous gasses. People died in their homes and in the streets without warning; their homes, businesses, and belongings were all buried with them. The ash hardened around the objects so that when archaeologists uncovered them nearly 1500 years later, they were able to see houses, furnishings, art, food, clothing, toys, and even people just as they were on the day they were buried.

Lesson 1—American Culture Mind Map Part I

Objective

Students will evaluate an aspect of American culture and then identify the category to which it belongs on the American Culture Mind Map.

Materials

Large piece of butcher paper or newsprint (a blank bulletin board will also work) • chalkboard or overhead projector • Mind Map Key • one copy of Mind Map bubbles #1 & #2 for bulletin board display • one Mind Map bubble #3 for each pair of students • one copy of Bubbles (Blanks) to be used for #4 bubbles for each pair of students • American Culture Homework page (Optional. One copy for each student.)

PREPARATION: Before this lesson, cut out bubbles labelled #1 and #2. Each bubble will need to be enlarged on a copy machine about 200% to get the appropriate size. Attach the bubbles to the butcher paper as shown on the Mind Map Key. Use a felt tip pen or crayon to draw the lines connecting the bubbles as shown. Cut out bubbles for students labelled #3, and enlarge about 200%.

As preparation for part II of this lesson, you may ask students to bring an everyday object from home. Ideally, there should be one per student. Almost anything will work as long as it is a common object. You may choose to provide an assortment of objects instead.

Critical Thinking Skills

• Analysis

• Evaluation

Step One: Introducing the Lesson

Ask students what they know about China (or any other country, except the U.S., that they may be familiar with). List their ideas on the chalkboard or overhead projector. (If necessary, prompt them with questions about dress, housing, transportation, holidays, or religion.) Keep this very short and simple—about five minutes. Explain to students that they have just described part of China's culture. Explain that culture is the attitudes, beliefs, customs, art, and achievements of a group of people. Students will spend the next several class periods studying American culture.

Step Two: Guided Practice

Divide students into pairs. Show students the butcher paper with the first two levels of the Mind Map in place.

Distribute one Mind Map #3 bubble and one copy of #4 bubbles to each pair of students. (If the class is small and there are more questions than students, make sure that at least two questions in each area are used. You may also elect to give out more than one question per team.)

Explain that the class is going to examine American culture by answering the question(s) on the Level #3 bubbles. Each pair of students is going to contribute to the American Culture Mind Map by brainstorming four answers to the question on their page. When students are finished, they will cut out their bubbles. If they have time, students may illustrate their answers.

Step Three: Guided Practice (cont.)

After students finish, allow time for them to share answers with the class. (The answers could potentially generate lengthy discussions. If time is a consideration, set a time limit for discussion of each question before students begin to share.) Before adding their bubble to the Mind Map, ask the class which part of culture the answers represent.

The teacher will collect the Mind Map #3 & #4 bubbles and place them on the bulletin board in the same position as shown on the Mind Map Key. Draw a line (with a crayon or thick felt tip pen) from the appropriate level 2 bubble to each level 3 bubble that is related to it. (See Mind Map Key.)

Lesson 1—American Culture Mind Map Part II

Objective

Students will evaluate artifacts, draw conclusions from the artifacts about American culture, and then categorize which aspect of American culture it addresses (achievements, beliefs, customs, arts, and attitudes).

Materials

Variety of artifacts • American Culture Mind Map (bulletin board from part 1) • bar of soap • bottle of dish soap • can of cleanser • Artifacts and Culture worksheet and Artifacts of American Culture worksheet (one copy per student) • #5 bubbles (one bubble per student)

Step One: Introduction Part II

Tell students about how the city of Pompeii was buried by volcanic ash and preserved. Ask students to imagine that their city was buried like Pompeii. When the city is excavated, archaeologists find that every house contains an average of three to five different kinds of soap for different purposes. (Show soap bottles.) Ask students what they think the archaeologists would be able to tell about the people. (They are obsessively clean. They know that cleanliness prevents disease. Most diseases in their civilization are not caused by uncleanliness. They don't believe that illnesses are caused by angry gods.)

Step Two: Guided Practice

Divide students into groups of 4. Distribute Artifacts and Culture worksheet to each student. Ask students to look at the artifacts in the first box. Ask them to work in their groups and think of one or two things the artifacts might tell them about the group of people they are studying. Allow several minutes for discussion. Ask for ideas from those students who came up with ideas—accept anything reasonable. For students who are not able to come up with ideas, ask them to write down some ideas that were presented by other groups. Ask students to identify which aspect(s) of culture was described by the group (beliefs, attitudes, customs, achievements, or art) and to mark those aspects that apply in the box in the center column of their worksheet. Repeat this process with the remaining artifacts.

Step Three: Independent Practice

Distribute the Artifacts of American Culture worksheet. Ask students to set the artifacts they brought in the middle of the group. (If you provided all the artifacts, distribute these artifacts to the groups.) Each student will write the name of the artifact in the Artifact column. Each group will discuss and arrive at a decision as to what each artifact would tell archaeologists about American culture. If their answer cannot be found in one of the #4 bubbles, suggest they add a bubble to the Mind Map. Students should then categorize their findings into attitudes, beliefs, customs, achievements, or art.

Step Four: Independent Practice (cont.)

Students will add their artifacts to the American Culture Mind Map. They may do this by attaching the actual artifact (if possible), by drawing a picture of the artifact in the #5 bubble, or by finding a picture of the artifact in a magazine and gluing it to a #5 bubble. The teacher may choose one of these methods or allow the students to choose. The #5 bubbles should then be added to the Map and lines drawn to connect them to the appropriate #4 bubble.

NOTE: Hold on to the American Culture Mind Map Bulletin Board. It will be added to in Unit 4.

Step Five: Closure

Begin with Attitudes on the American Culture Mind Map. Ask those students who connected their #5 bubbles to Attitudes to report to the class about their artifact and what the artifact told them about American culture. Students should be able to explain why their artifact should be connected to the Attitudes bubble. You may want to set a time limit on discussions before beginning. After each artifact connected to Attitudes has been discussed, move to the next category and repeat the process. As each #4 bubble is completed, ask if there are any artifacts other than those brought in that might help archaeologists tell about that part of American culture.

Lesson 2—The Culture of the Dig

Objective

Students will make reasonable assumptions about the culture of the people by examining the artifacts they found during Unit 1.

Materials

Field Record Pages and Field-Square Plan from Unit 1 • Culture of the Dig worksheet (one per student)

Critical Thinking Skills

- Analysis
- Inductive reasoning
- Application

Step One: Introducing the Lesson

Teacher Script: *You have had a lot of practice making conclusions about a culture based on the artifacts. This time you will have a chance to work on your own. You will look back at the information that you gathered during the dig in Unit 1 and draw conclusions about the culture of the people that left those artifacts.*

Step Two: Guided Practice

Ask students to take out the Field Record Pages and Field-Square Plan from the archaeological dig. Distribute the Culture of the Dig worksheet. Students will look at the artifacts they drew during their dig. They will draw conclusions about the achievements, customs, beliefs, attitudes, and art of the people they studied and record the information on the Culture of the Dig worksheet. Ask students to look at the Artifacts/Objects box next to the Achievements box. Ask them, *What possible achievements would the artifacts indicate?* Possible answers: They knew how to weave cloth and use natural things to make dyes. They developed a system of writing and recorded important events. They knew how to make boats. They learned how to weave baskets from grass.

Step Three: Independent Practice

Students will complete the remainder of the worksheet independently. This activity can be either an individual or group activity and can be used as an assessment of the skills learned in this unit.

Mind Map Key

Directions: Place each student's completed #3 & #4 bubbles on the bulletin board and draw a line to connect them to the corresponding #2 bubble. Place each student's completed #5 bubble on the bulletin board and draw a line to connect it to the corresponding #4 bubble. Below is an abbreviated example of what the American Culture Mind Map should look like.

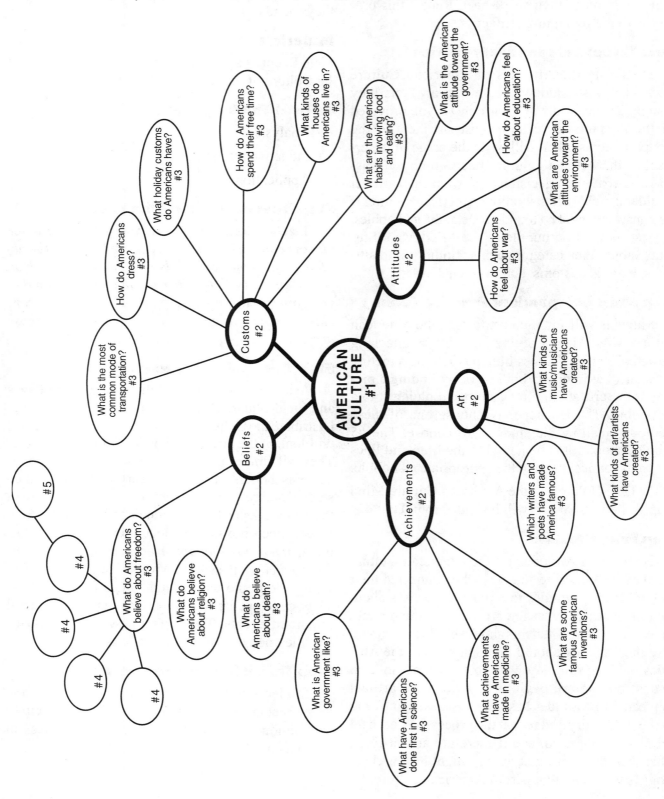

Bubbles #1, #2, and #3

(Cut on lines and enlarge approximately 200%.)

AMERICAN
CULTURE
#1

How do
Americans
feel about war?
#3

What holiday
customs do
Americans have?
#3

ACHIEVEMENTS
#2

What are American
attitudes toward the
environment?
#3

How do
Americans dress?
#3

ATTITUDES
#2

How do Americans
feel about
education?
#3

What is the most
common mode of
transportation?
#3

BELIEFS
#2

What is the
American attitude
toward the
government?
#3

What have
Americans done
first in science?
#3

CUSTOMS
#2

What are the
American habits
involving food and
eating?
#3

What do Americans
believe about death?
#3

ART
#2

What do
Americans
believe about
religion?
#3

What is
American
government like?
#3

What kinds of
music/musicians
have Americans
created?
#3

What kind of houses
do Americans live
in?
#3

What achievements
have Americans
made in medicine?
#3

What do
Americans believe
about freedom?
#3

How do Americans
spend their free
time?
#3

What are some
famous American
inventions?
#3

What kinds of
art/artists
have Americans
created?
#3

Which writers and
poets have made
America famous?
#3

Bubbles (Blanks)

(Use these bubbles for #4 and #5 bubbles.)

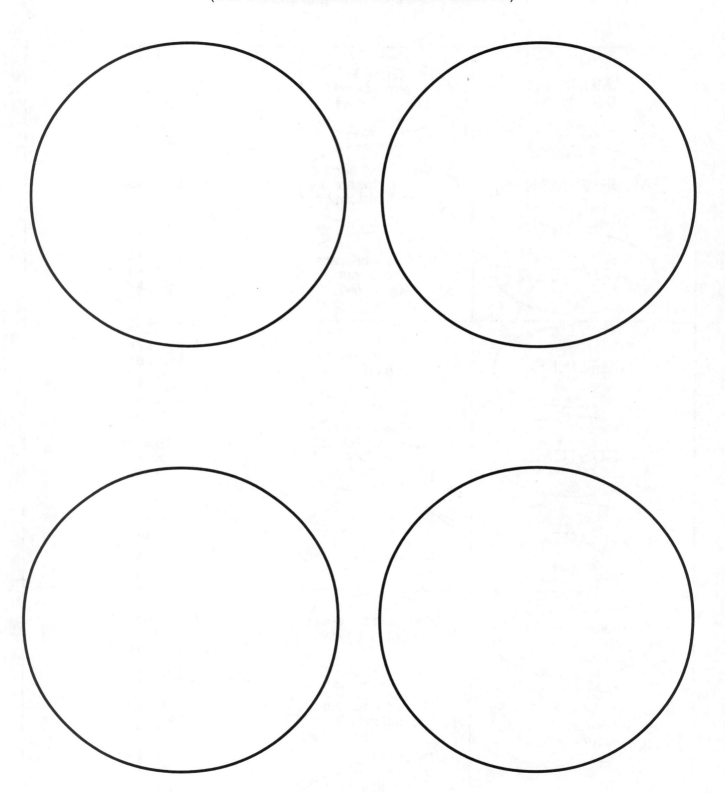

American Culture Homework

Name _____

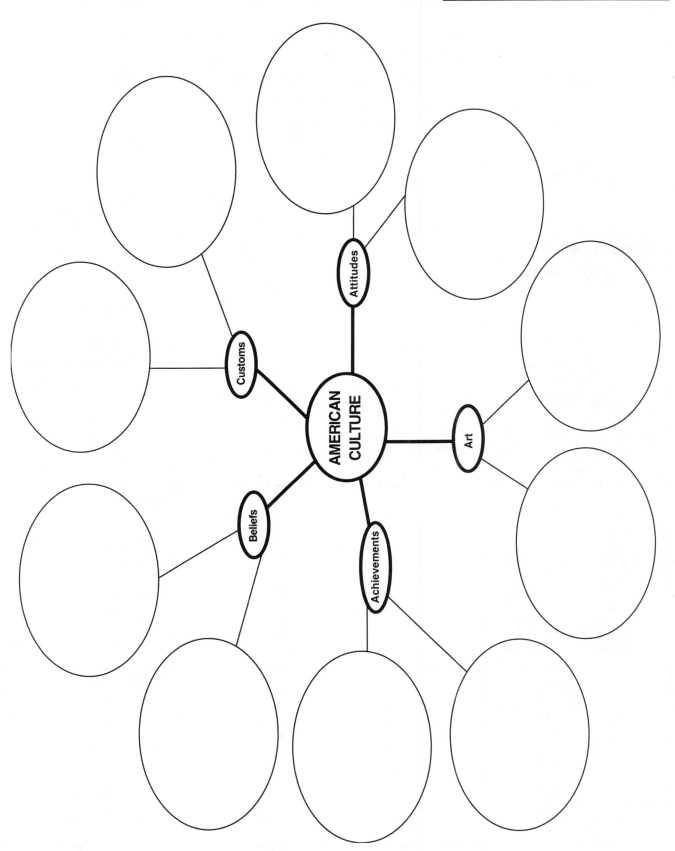

Artifacts and Culture

Name _____

ARTIFACT	WHAT DOES IT TELL ABOUT THE CULTURE OF THESE PEOPLE?	ATTRIBUTES
	1	Check the attributes that apply: ☐ Achievements ☐ Customs ☐ Beliefs ☐ Attitudes ☐ Art
	2	Check the attributes that apply: ☐ Achievements ☐ Customs ☐ Beliefs ☐ Attitudes ☐ Art
	3	Check the attributes that apply: ☐ Achievements ☐ Customs ☐ Beliefs ☐ Attitudes ☐ Art
	4	Check the attributes that apply: ☐ Achievements ☐ Customs ☐ Beliefs ☐ Attitudes ☐ Art

Artifacts of American Culture

Name _____

ARTIFACT	WHAT DOES IT TELL ABOUT THE CULTURE OF THESE PEOPLE?	ATTRIBUTES
	1	Check the attributes that apply: ☐ Achievements ☐ Customs ☐ Beliefs ☐ Attitudes ☐ Art
	2	Check the attributes that apply: ☐ Achievements ☐ Customs ☐ Beliefs ☐ Attitudes ☐ Art
	3	Check the attributes that apply: ☐ Achievements ☐ Customs ☐ Beliefs ☐ Attitudes ☐ Art
	4	Check the attributes that apply: ☐ Achievements ☐ Customs ☐ Beliefs ☐ Attitudes ☐ Art

Culture of the Dig

Name _____

ACHIEVEMENTS	ARTIFACTS/OBJECTS
	1. Woven, dyed cloth 2. Scrolls with writing on them 3. Canoe 4. Woven baskets
CUSTOMS	**ARTIFACTS/OBJECTS**
	1. Rock path leading to ocean 2. Number of shells outside each house 3. Seashells, seaweed, grains in midden 4. Fire pit in center of village 5. Tan cloth 6. Fish nets
BELIEFS	**ARTIFACTS/OBJECTS**
	1. Human skeleton wrapped in red cloth 2. Human skeleton buried with dolphin mask and covered with seaweed 3. Red spindle found only in largest house 4. No animal remains found in midden 5. No animal skins used in homes or as clothing
ATTITUDES	**ARTIFACTS/OBJECTS**
	1. Written scrolls found only in the largest house 2. Weaving looms and fishing nets found in every house 3. No weapons of any kind found 4. Games
ART	**ARTIFACTS/OBJECTS**
	1. Woven baskets 2. Woven cloth 3. Dolphin masks 4. Carved figures in game

UNIT 4
WHAT IS A CIVILIZATION?

Chapter 1
Stable Food Supply

Background Information

A civilization is a group of people who have reached an advanced stage of social, political, and cultural development. Their social structure includes a stable food supply and specialization of labor. They have an organized system of government that allows them to complete large projects and gather armies to defend the civilization against intruders. A civilization also has all the recognizable traits inherent in culture—achievements in science and the arts, beliefs, customs, and attitudes.

A stable food supply is necessary in order for a civilization to develop and grow. If a population must always worry about providing food for its members, it will not have time to create art, invent, or write—survival will be the first priority. Therefore, when archaeologists are looking for evidence of a stable food supply, the presence of sculptures, paintings, and writings is a strong indicator that the people had a stable food supply.

A stable food supply usually indicates that plants and animals have been domesticated. The process of domestication involves the taming of wild plants and animals for agricultural purposes. When people domesticate crops and animals, they no longer have to spend their days walking miles through the wilderness, gleaning wild plants when they can find them, and hoping to find game to trap and kill. Crops and animals are located in one place, which allows for more time and increased food production. With more time, people can dramatically increase their food production. In fact, one person can raise a surplus (more than one household can use). Given a surplus of food, it is unnecessary for every household to farm, and people can explore other specialties. These specialties spawn new commodities that can then be traded for food and vice versa.

Lesson 1—Hunter-Gatherers vs. Farmers

Objective

Students will demonstrate an understanding of the advantages of an agricultural society over a hunter-gatherer society in the development of a civilization by writing two paragraphs about the advantages of agriculture in the development of a civilization.

Materials

Each group will need a bowl, cup, or plastic bags; crayons or colored pencils; scissors; tape or glue • Food Supply Project Page and Stable Food Supply worksheet (one of each for each student) • Teacher will need 2 cups of uncooked beans, 2 tablespoons, and 2 bowls

Critical Thinking Skills

- Analysis
- Synthesis
- Inductive reasoning

Step One: Introducing the Lesson

Divide the beans into two bowls. Place a tablespoon in each bowl. Label one bowl "Hunter-Gatherers" and the other "Agricultural." Place them in two different places in the room where students will be able to form a line near them. Divide the students into groups of four. Distribute Food Supply Project Page (one for each student). Distribute a bowl, cup, or plastic bag to each group. Prepare a sample of the building on the Food Supply Project page for students to see.

Teacher Script: *Today you are going to play a game called Food Supply. Your groups will be called tribes. Some groups will be hunter-gatherer tribes, and some groups will be agricultural tribes.*

In ancient times, before there were villages and cities, people did not stay in one place for very long.

They did not know how to plant seeds to grow plants or domesticate animals for food. The only way to get food was to pick wild fruit, vegetables, and roots or to hunt or trap wild animals in the area. After the tribe had been in an area for a while, they would eat more food than the land could provide, or the herds of animals would migrate and food would become scarce. The tribe would then pack up their belongings and move to a place where they could find more food. These tribes are called hunter-gatherers because nearly all their time is spent hunting and gathering food.

Agricultural tribes are groups of people who plant crops and raise animals for food. They do not move as often as hunter-gatherer tribes.

There are two objects to this game. The first object is to keep your tribe supplied with food so that they will not starve. The second object of the game is to help your tribe build a civilization with the greatest buildings.

Each team has a (bowl, cup, or bag). When you gather food so that your tribe can survive, you will put it in your container. Each person in your tribe needs 2 tablespoons of food every year to survive. If your team is a hunter-gatherer tribe, every person in the team must get in line and each person must get his/her own food into the container. If your team is an agricultural tribe, one person from the tribe will be appointed as the farmer, and the farmer will get enough food for the whole tribe. You will go to get food every time you hear me say, "Food!" When I say "Food," the food gatherers will form a single file line by the correct food supply. Hunter-gatherers will line up by the hunter-gatherer's food supply. (Show students where this is located.) Farmers from the agricultural tribe will line up by the agricultural food supply. (Show students where this is located.)

When the members of your tribe are not gathering food, they should be coloring and constructing the building. You want to get as much of the building built as possible.

Designate each group hunter-gatherer or agricultural. (Approximately half of the groups should be hunter-gatherers and half should be agricultural.) To make sure that students understand who should get the food and where they should go, call "Food" and let students do a practice run.

Tell students to begin their projects. Allow 3–4 minutes for them to start before calling "Food!" One minute after the last hunter-gatherer collects his food, call "Food!" again. After all the teams have collected their food for this round, move the hunter-gatherer food supply. Do not tell them that it has been moved and do not point out its location. Call "Food!" again. Continue to follow this same pattern until it appears that most of the agricultural tribes (with the exception of the farmers) are finished with their projects. Then tell students that the game is over and instruct them to stop their work.

Step Two: Guided Practice

Distribute Stable Food Supply worksheet. Guide students through questions 1 and 2. Ask students to observe projects made by agricultural tribes. Then ask students to observe projects made by hunter-gatherer tribes (questions 4 & 5). After discussing the students' observations, discuss the answers to 5, 6, and 7.

Step Three: Independent Practice

Students should complete questions 8–13 of the Stable Food Supply worksheet independently.

Step Four: Closure

Students will write two paragraphs expressing the advantages of agriculture in the development of a civilization. Students should make sure that they use the words *hunter-gatherer, agriculture, supply,* and *surplus.*

Lesson 2—Domestication

Objective

Students will identify the level of domestication in a society by studying the remains of its food.

Materials

Overhead projector • Domestication #1 and Domestication #2—Seeds (one of each per student) • make a transparency of Transparency—Domestication • calipers • ruler or protractor

Critical Thinking Skills

• Inductive reasoning

• Analysis

• Synthesis

Step One: Introducing the Lesson

Teacher Script: *You have already learned that agriculture allowed people to begin building large civilizations. Today you are going to get a chance to find out how archaeologists determine how much food people are getting from farming and how much they are getting by hunting and gathering.*

Step Two: Acquiring Information

Place the Transparency—Domestication on overhead projector. Cover entire page except row A. Tell students they are hunters and gatherers from the days of the cave people and that they are going to try to become farmers.

Ask students where they would get the seeds and animals to start their farm. (Catch wild animals, collect wild plants)

Show students row A. Tell them that these are the wild birds and the seeds from the wild plants. Ask them to identify which seeds they would want to use to plant next year's crop and which birds they would like to keep to have next year's baby birds. (The biggest ones. *Why?* The farmer gets more food for less work.)

Show students row B. Tell them that a year has passed and that these are the seeds from the new plants they planted last year. Explain to students that these birds are the chicks of the birds they kept for breeding last year. Repeat the process from row A. (Students should choose the largest seeds and birds.)

Repeat the entire discussion for rows C and D. When this is finished, ask students to observe the difference in size between the wild seeds and birds and the domestic seeds and birds. Tell them that this is how archaeologists distinguish wild seeds, plant remains, and animal skeletons from domestic ones. Explain that the process of domestication they observed may actually take 50 years or longer to complete.

Ask students to think about this question: *If archaeologists find a village with only wild seeds, plants, and animal remains, what does this tell them about the life-style of the people in the village?* (They gather what they can—they move from place to place as they find food. Their villages are probably temporary. Their homes are probably those that can be moved or rebuilt easily. They probably have few personal belongings.)

Then ask students to answer this question: *If archaeologists find a village with only domestic seeds, plants, and animal remains, what does it tell about the people's life-style?* (They are probably farmers who have stayed in the same place for a long time. Their homes are probably larger and more permanent. The houses may stay in the family for generations, so they are decorated and cluttered with accumulated belongings. There may be some people in the village who do not raise any food at all, but trade with farmers to get what they want.) *This specialization of labor can happen only when there is a stable food supply. A stable food supply means the people have learned how to domesticate plants and animals.*

What if they find both? (They are probably in the process of domesticating plants and/or animals. They still depend on hunting and gathering for some of their food supply. If there are very few wild ones, they may be naturally occurring and not gathered by the people at all.)

Step Three: Guided Practice

Distribute Domestication #1 worksheet.

Teacher Script: *You are going to look at some seeds that were found in middens and determine the amount of agriculture that was present in this civilization. Look at the seeds in the top box. You will notice that there are three different kinds—wheat seeds, pumpkin seeds, and corn seeds. The first thing that an archaeologist would do is sort the seeds by type. Notice each seed has a number. You will sort these seeds by writing the numbers of the wheat seeds on the wheat seed blank, the pumpkin seeds on the pumpkin seed blank, and the corn seeds on the corn seed blank. Then you will decide which of the seeds are from wild plants and which of the seeds are from domestic plants. Lightly shade in the domestic seeds with your pencil. Write the numbers of the wild seeds in the boxes labeled wild seeds. Write the numbers of the domestic seeds in the boxes labeled domestic seeds. Measure the length of each seed using your calipers and record its length next to its number.*

Add up the measurements for the wild seeds. Then add up the measurements for the domestic seeds. Record the totals for each one in the appropriate Total Length columns. Find the average length of a seed (wild and domestic) by dividing the total length by the total number of seeds. Write your results on the line marked Average.

Distribute Domestication #2—Seeds worksheet. Students follow the directions at the top of the page to compute the number of degrees that will be allowed for each part of the pie graph. You may want to do this with the students. Students will use a protractor to mark the proportions in the circle. They will shade the key and the appropriate portions of the pie graph.

Step Four: Independent Practice

Students complete Section B, questions 1–4, on the Domestication #2—Seeds worksheet independently.

Step Five: Closure

Draw the circle graph below on the chalk board. On the back of the Domestication #2 worksheet, students will write down five characteristics of this society.

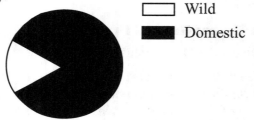

☐ Wild
■ Domestic

CLOSURE (Possible answers):

1. They are an agricultural society.
2. They have learned to domesticate plants and animals.
3. Some of them are farmers.
4. They are not a mobile society.
5. They probably built stationary houses.
6. They had time to create art and literature.

7. They lived in larger groups.
8. They had time to collect more personal possessions.

Bulletin Board

On the right side of the bulletin board containing your American Culture Mind Map or on a second sheet of craft paper placed on the right side of the Mind Map, place the large rectangle with the word "Civilization" printed on it. Draw a line connecting the "Civilization" rectangle with the "American Culture" bubble. Cut out the "Social Structure" bubble. Place it above right of the "Civilization" rectangle. Connect them with a line. Place the "Specialization of Labor" square and the "Stable Food Supply" square above the "Social Structure" bubble, and connect them with a line. Cut out the "Government" bubble, and place it below right of the "Civilization" square. See the Civilization Mind Map Key below.

Cut out bubbles below and enlarge approximately 530%.

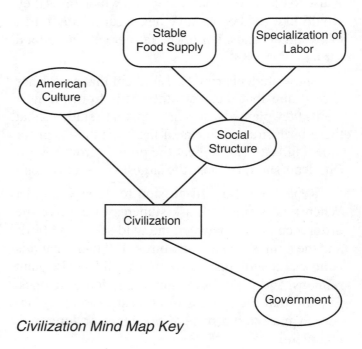

Civilization Mind Map Key

Food Supply Project Page

Directions: The castle below is actually two buildings. First, color the top two sections. Then cut the top sections out. Fold each one along the vertical lines. Fold the tiled roof sections back slightly. Place glue on the white strips of each building and glue the white strips together to form a rectangular building. Color the bottom building. Cut out the bottom building. Fold along the four vertical lines. Place glue on the white strip and glue together to form a building. Last, glue side A of the top building to side B of the bottom building.

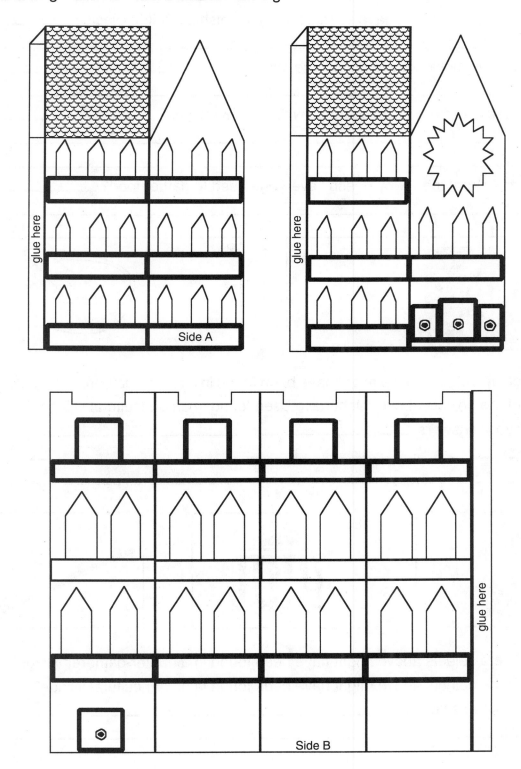

Stable Food Supply

Name _____

1. What is agriculture? _____

2. What are hunter-gatherers? _____

3. Which tribes finished their projects first? _____

4. Why did the other tribes have so much trouble finishing their projects? _____
   _____

5. Which tribe is more likely to build large towns? _____
   Why? _____

6. Which tribe is more likely to come up with new inventions? _____
   _____
   Why? _____

7. In an agricultural tribe, why doesn't everyone need to gather food? _____
   _____

A.

B.

8. Which of the objects above might have been found in a hunter-gatherer village? _____

9. Which of the objects above might have been found in an agricultural village? _____

10. Explain your answers. _____
    _____
    _____

A.

B.

C.

11. Which of the objects above might have been found in a hunter-gatherer village? _____

12. Which of the objects above might have been found in an agricultural village? _____

13. Explain your answers. _____
    _____

Transparency—Domestication

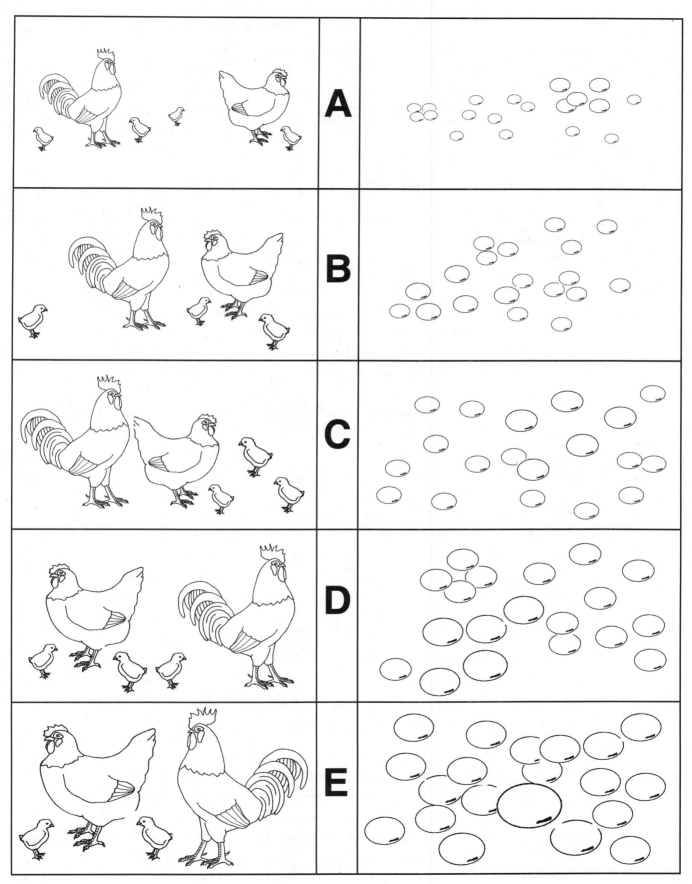

Domestication #1

Name _____

Directions: Measure the length of each seed using your calipers.

Wheat Seed Numbers:

Wild		Domestic	
Seed #	Length	Seed #	Length
Total Length:		Total Length:	
Average:		Average:	

Pumpkin Seed Numbers:

Wild		Domestic	
Seed #	Length	Seed #	Length
Total Length:		Total Length:	
Average:		Average:	

Corn Seed Numbers:

Wild		Domestic	
Seed #	Length	Seed #	Length
Total Length:		Total Length:	
Average:		Average:	

Domestication #2—Seeds

Name _____

A.

Directions: From the information that you gathered by sorting and measuring the seeds from the midden, you are going to draw a circle graph to show the amount of domestic seeds and the amount of wild seeds found.

1. Add the total number of seeds in box A. _____
2. Add the total number of domestic seeds of all types. _____
3. Add the total number of wild seeds of all types. _____
4. Divide the total number of domestic seeds by the total number of seeds. _____
5. Divide the total number of wild seeds by the total number of seeds. _____
6. Multiply the answer to #4 by 360° (degrees in a circle). _____
7. Multiply the answer to #5 by 360° (degrees in a circle). _____
8. Using a protractor, mark off the number of degrees (from #6 and #7) on the circle below. Color the key and then color the circle graph.

☐ Wild

☐ Domestic

B.

1. Was this society mostly agricultural or hunter-gatherer? _____
2. How do you know? _____

   _____

3. Describe how the wild pumpkin seeds in box A became the size of the domestic seeds.

   _____

   _____

   _____

   _____

4. Would this society migrate often? _____   Explain your answer. _____

   _____

   _____

Chapter 2
Specialization of Labor (Level of Technology)

Background Information

The complexity of a civilization can be gauged by examining the degree of specialization in its labor force. For example, a carpenter of today does not cut his own trees to make his boards or even deliver the boards to the building site. He does not put the roof on the house or install the plumbing or lay the carpet. His job is very specific: he cuts boards to their proper length and nails them together.

Lesson 1—Four Walls

Objective

Students will critically observe pictures of artifacts and deduce the technological levels of the civilizations represented by the knowledge, skills, and tools and materials used in their construction.

Materials

Four Walls worksheet and Level of Technology—Transportation worksheet (one copy of each for each student)

Critical Thinking Skills

- Inference
- Synthesis
- Deductive reasoning

Step One: Introducing the Lesson

Distribute the Four Walls worksheet. Tell students that an archaeologist was studying four walls from four different buildings that were found in four different strata. The archaeologist made a drawing of each of the walls. Students can see the drawings by looking at their worksheet.

Step Two: Guided Practice

Divide the students into groups of four. Ask them to discuss the four drawings with the other people in their group. Ask groups to begin by describing the walls. This will help them focus on details. Next, ask them to focus on the questions below each wall.

Discuss answers and observations as a class. Ask students to decide which of the walls was the most difficult to make. Tell them to label this wall #1. Ask them to keep their answers private until it is time to discuss them. Next, ask them to choose the second most difficult wall to build and label it #2. Label the third most difficult #3. Label the easiest to build #4. Discuss the students' answers. Ask students to justify their answers.

Step Three: Independent Practice

Distribute the Level of Technology—Transportation worksheet. Students will complete the Level of Technology worksheet independently.

Lesson 2—Give Me a Shirt

Objective

Students will diagram the levels of specialization of labor involved in the manufacture of a particular artifact. Students will tell why specialization of labor is necessary for the development of a civilization.

Materials

Cotton-type shirt with buttons • large piece of craft paper • handful of dirt • Specialization of Labor Diagram worksheet (two per student) • clock • several complex, manufactured objects made of at least two materials (lamp, pencil, sewing machine, overhead projector, camera, doll, screwdriver, etc.)

Critical Thinking Skills

- Inference
- Deductive reasoning
- Synthesis

Step One: Introducing the Lesson

Show students a shirt (cotton-type with buttons). Ask students to make a guess as to how many people it takes to produce a shirt they buy in the store. Accept all guesses with neutral comments. Record the guesses on the chalkboard.

Explain that the class is going to take a closer look at the problem to see if they can come up with a more precise answer to the question.

Hang the large piece of craft paper in the front of the room. Pose the following questions to the class one at a time. (Student answers may vary from those given here.) As students answer, write the answers on the craft paper with a heavy marker. Use the Give Me A Shirt Diagram at the end of this lesson as your guide. This activity is only an introduction to the idea and is not meant to take a long time. Move through the process as quickly as possible.

1. *Who sold you the shirt?* Salesperson

2. *Who put the shirt on the shelf?* Stock person

3. *Who bought the shirt for the store?* Owner

4. *Who delivered the shirt to the owner?* Truck driver

5. *Who sewed the shirt?* Shirt factory workers (cutters, designers, seamstresses)

6. *Where did the factory get the fabric?* Fabric salesperson

7. *Who made the fabric?* Fabric factory workers (cleaners, combers, weavers, dyers)

8. *Who provided the factory with the raw materials?* Cotton farmer

9. *Where does the cotton farmer get his/her tractor and other equipment?* Farm equipment salesperson

10. *Who makes the farm equipment?* Farm equipment factory workers

11. *Who provides water for the crops?* Irrigation workers

12. *Who provides pesticides for the crops?* Pesticide factory workers

13. *Who provided the buttons for the shirt?* Button salesperson

14. *Who made buttons?* Button factory workers

15. *Who provided raw materials for the buttons?* Plastics manufacturers

16. *Who delivered the raw materials for the buttons to the factory?* Truck/train drivers

17. *Where did the shirt factory get the thread to sew the shirts?* Thread salesperson

18. *Where did the thread salesperson get the thread?* Thread factory workers

19. *Where did the factory get its machines?* Machinery salesperson

20. *Who made the machines?* Tool manufacturers

21. *Who built the truck for the truck driver?* Truck factory workers

22. *Who provided the metal for the parts?* Metal foundry workers

23. *Who provided the raw materials for the foundries?* Miners

24. *Who provided the plastic parts of the truck?* Plastic parts salesperson

25. *Who made the plastic parts?* Plastic molding factory workers

26. *Who provided the plastic?* Plastics manufacturing workers

27. *Who manufactured the controls?* Controls manufacturers

TEACHER SCRIPT: *The number of people involved in making one shirt is more than anyone expected, isn't it? Each person on this chart has a specific job to do. Would you expect the sales clerk in the store to sew your shirt?* (This may sound so ridiculous to them that they laugh.) *Does the person who works in the button factory farm cotton?* (Not likely) *When it takes several different people to do several different jobs, you have what is called Specialization of Labor.*

Specialization is necessary for a civilization to develop because one person cannot have enough time to make all of the things he/she uses every day. (Hold out a handful of dirt to the students.) *This dirt contains iron ore. How many of you could make a toaster from it? Why not?* (Don't have the skills, knowledge, or tools.)

Look at the chart. How many of these people grow food for a living? (None) *How do they get food to eat?* (They get their food from stores that get it from farmers.) *Why do the farmers have food to give them?* (They raise a surplus food supply. They've domesticated plants and animals.) *You cannot have very much specialization of labor without agriculture. Why?* (Because you must be able to eat before you consider doing anything else.) *How much specialization of labor would you expect a hunter-gatherer society to have?* (Little or none) *Why?* (They are spending all their time hunting and gathering food.)

Add up the number of people necessary to make it possible for you to buy this shirt in the store. When we buy a shirt, we do not consider all the people that are involved. Our level of technology is very high. Every job requires manufactured tools, most require electricity, and nearly all require some specialized knowledge. The people in the jobs have to be trained to use the tools.

Think about a cave person's tunic. What is a cave person's clothing made of? (animal skins of some kind) *Who gives the cave person the animal skins?* (No one. The cave person goes out and hunts for them.) *Is there any specialization of labor?* (No. Jobs are interchangeable. The cave person does every job. The cave person has a very low level of technology. He/she requires very few tools and little knowledge to obtain his/her clothing.)

Step Two: Guided Practice

Divide students into groups of four. Distribute the Specialization of Labor Diagram worksheet. Place the clock in front of the class. Explain that it was found in an archaeological dig and that they are to determine how many levels of specialization of labor were present in the civilization by drawing a diagram similar to the one they just saw on the craft paper. Then students will answer the questions at the

bottom of the page. Check students' progress as they complete this assignment. Use the word list below to guide students through the activity.

- clock factory workers
- lumbermill workers
- lumberjacks
- gear manufacturing factory workers
- metal foundry workers
- miners
- plastic manufacturing company workers
- chemical company workers
- delivery truck drivers
- truck manufacturers

Step Three: Independent Practice

Distribute a second copy of the Specialization of Labor Diagram worksheet. Ask students to choose one artifact from the dig that they completed in Unit 1. Working independently, they will diagram the specialization of labor needed to manufacture the object and answer the questions at the bottom of the page.

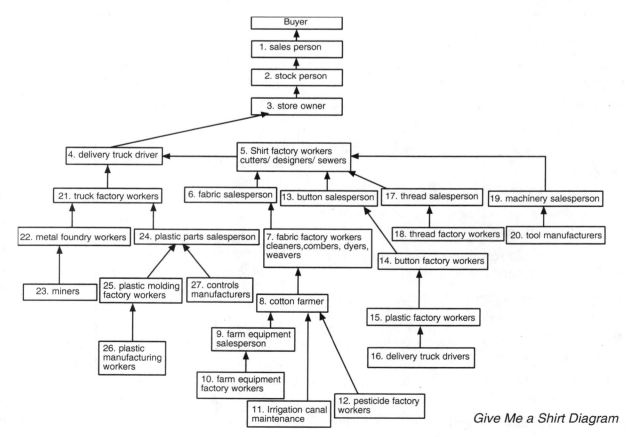

Give Me a Shirt Diagram

Four Walls

Name _____

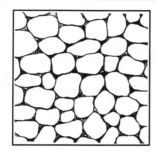

1. Describe the wall above. _____
_____

2. What tools and materials were needed to build it? _____
_____

3. What knowledge and skills were required?
_____
_____

4. What types of people were most likely in-volved in making the tools, supplies, and the wall itself? _____
_____
_____

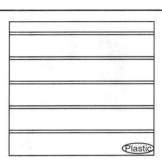

Plastic

1. Describe the wall above. _____
_____

2. What tools and materials were needed to build it? _____
_____

3. What knowledge and skills were required?
_____
_____

4. What types of people were most likely in-volved in making the tools, supplies, and the wall itself? _____
_____
_____

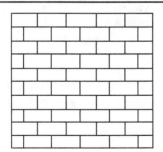

1. Describe the wall above. _____
_____

2. What tools and materials were needed to build it? _____
_____

3. What knowledge and skills were required?
_____
_____

4. What types of people were most likely in-volved in making the tools, supplies, and the wall itself? _____
_____
_____

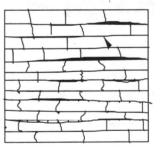

1. Describe the wall above. _____
_____

2. What tools and materials were needed to build it? _____
_____

3. What knowledge and skills were required?
_____
_____

4. What types of people were most likely in-volved in making the tools, supplies, and the wall itself? _____
_____
_____

Level of Technology—Transportation

Name _____

A

What tools and materials were required to build, acquire, or maintain this type of transportation?

_____
_____
_____

What knowledge and skills were required?

_____
_____

B

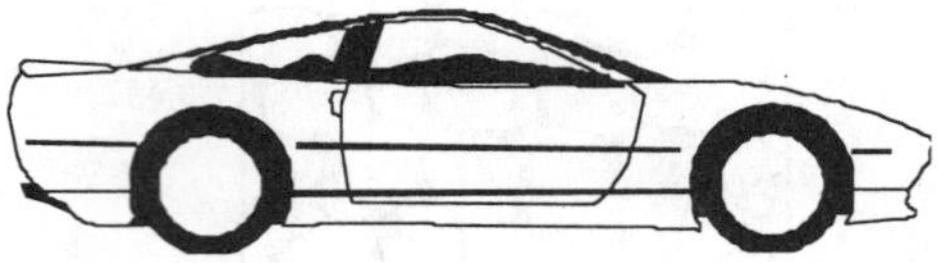

What tools and materials were required to build, acquire, or maintain this type of transportation?

_____
_____
_____

What knowledge and skills were required?

_____
_____

C

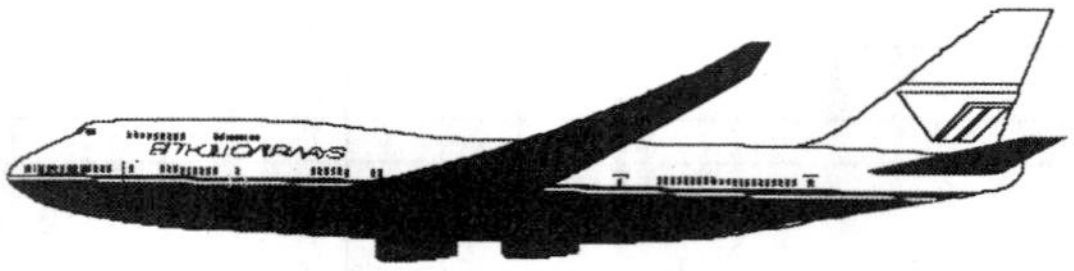

What tools and materials were required to build, acquire, or maintain this type of transportation?

_____
_____
_____

What knowledge and skills were required?

_____
_____

D

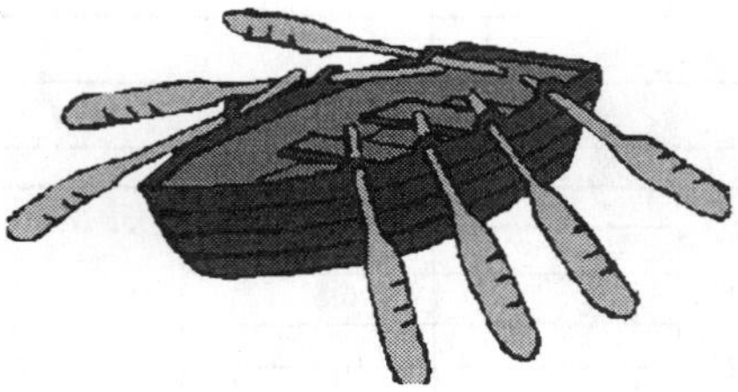

What tools and materials were required to build, acquire, or maintain this type of transportation?

_____
_____
_____

What knowledge and skills were required?

_____
_____

---

1. Rank the cultures illustrated above according to their level of technology.

_____   _____   _____   _____

    (highest)   (lowest)

2. Why did you place them in the order that you did?

3. What would prevent the culture with the lowest technology from building an airplane?

© 1999 Critical Thinking Books & Software • www.criticalthinking.com • (800)458-4849

Specialization of Labor Diagram

Name _____

Directions: Use the diagram below to determine how many levels of specialization of labor were present in the civilization.

1. How many levels of specialized jobs did you find? _____

2. How do people who are doing these specialized jobs get their food? _____

3. Would you rate the technology level of this civilization as low, medium, or high? _____

4. Why is there little or no specialization in a hunter-gatherer society? _____

5. Why is the beginning of agriculture necessary for specialization of labor? _____

Chapter 3
Government

Background Information

Civilization requires a government. This government may take a multitude of different forms, but there must be a person or group of persons who rule the society.

There are many indicators that can tell archaeologists about a civilization's government. One of the primary indicators is a large project that would require a massive work force and a high degree of organization and planning for the building and maintenance of the project. Some examples of such projects are irrigation projects, the pyramids in Egypt, the ziggurats in Babylon, and the roads of Rome.

Another indicator of the presence of a government is evidence of an organized military. A military must be assembled by a government—it does not assemble by itself. The evidence may take the form of a uniform, medals, or statues. A civilization needs to be able to defend itself against other civilizations so that it can continue to grow and develop.

Lesson 1—The King's House (Organizing Large Projects)

Objective

Students will determine whether a group of people had a government by looking at the size and complexity of large artifacts.

Materials

18 pieces of drawing paper (8 1/2 by 11 or larger, 2 pieces per group) • drawing tools • scissors • cellophane tape • The King's House worksheet and Government Projects worksheet (one copy per student) • Building Directions (one copy)

Critical Thinking Skills

- Evaluation
- Application
- Analysis

Step One: Introducing the Lesson

Divide students into nine small groups. Distrib-
ute one piece of drawing paper to each group. The students' task is to draw part of a wall of a huge house suitable for the king of their country. This is not just any house. This house takes up three city blocks and will require the work of nine different groups of people to complete. Each group may make their section any size, style, and color they wish. They may make it out of any materials they wish (draw the materials onto the paper). Students should color and cut out their section of the wall. They should not show or tell any other group anything about their wall. Set a time limit of five to ten minutes. Assign each group to a section of wall: first floor front, second floor front, first floor east, second floor east, first floor west, second floor west, first floor back, second floor back, roof.

Collect the finished walls and roof. Using your tape, assemble the walls on a table or flat surface at the front of the room. The walls will probably be a variety of different sizes, styles, and colors. It may be next to impossible to assemble it into anything that looks like a house. That's the point.

Distribute The King's House worksheet. At the top of the paper, ask students to quickly sketch the assembled house. Ask them to discuss and answer questions 2 through 4 as a group.

As a class, discuss the answers to questions 3 and 4. Tell them that a person or group of people who leads other people is called "government." This is the answer to question 4.

Step Two: Introduction (cont.)

Assign each group a number from 1 to 9. Cut the Building Directions worksheet into strips. Choose one student from the class to act as the government. He/she will distribute the second piece of white paper to each group. He/she will then distribute the strips of directions. Students need to know that they are receiving their directions from the government. As the student in charge distributes directions to each group, he/she should say to each group, "I am the government. Here are your building directions. You have ten minutes to finish."

When all the groups have finished their pieces, collect them. Using tape, the teacher will assemble the house on a level surface at the front of the classroom.

Working as a group, students will draw a picture of the second house and answer questions 6–8 on the King's House worksheet. Discuss the answers to questions 6–8 with students.

Step Three: Guided Practice

Students will remain in their groups to complete this activity. Distribute Government Projects worksheet. Ask students to pretend that they are living in ancient times in the dry lands near the Euphrates River. Tell them that their crops are a long distance from the river. Ask them to work as a group to come up with a way to get water to their crops all by themselves. Ask a volunteer from each group to provide the group's answer to the class. When all the groups are finished, draw a stick figure carrying a bucket of water from the river to the fields. Ask students to copy this into box A. (This is one of the few acceptable answers. If the students' answer is to dig a ditch to the plants, tell them that it takes all day to carry the water from the river and that if they take time to dig a ditch, the plants will die. This same reasoning applies if they choose to build some sort of apparatus.)

Now ask students to imagine that a government took charge of helping the people water their fields. Ask them to discuss what the government might do. As a class, share answers; accept anything reasonable. (Possible answers: drilling a well and then digging trenches to the fields or digging trenches from the river to the fields.) Choose one possible answer and draw it on the board. Students will draw their solution in box B. Label the first picture "without a government" and the second picture "with a government." Students should do the same with their worksheet. Discuss and answer questions 1 and 2 together.

Step Four: Independent Practice

In box C, labeled "without government," ask students to draw a picture of how a person might send a message from one side of a large town to another if there was no government. In box D, labeled "with a government," ask students to draw a picture of how a person might send a message if the government had developed a communications system. Students should answer questions 3, 4, and 5 independently.

Lesson 2—Building Defenses

Objective

Students will demonstrate an understanding of the necessity of government defense in the formation of a civilization by writing a paragraph about how they would divide the labor in the make-believe town, Hometown.

Materials

Hometown worksheet, Houses and Roads page, Crops and Roads page, and Government Defenses worksheet (one of each for each student) • one piece of tagboard (18 by 24 inches) and one roll of scotch tape (one of each for each group)

Critical Thinking Skills

- Analysis
- Synthesis
- Deductive reasoning
- Inference

Step One: Introducing the Lesson

Divide students into groups of four or five. Distribute Hometown worksheet, tagboard, Crops and Roads page, and Houses and Roads page. Ask students to cut out the people rectangles at the bottom of the Hometown worksheet. Each student in the group needs to choose a different crayon and color the clothing of all six of his/her townspeople with that particular color.

TEACHER SCRIPT: *Today, you are going to pretend that your group is a community that wants to build a town. This is a contest to see which group can build the most buildings, the most streets, and the biggest farms in ten minutes. Each building is worth ten points, each plant is worth three points, and each inch of road is worth seven points. These buildings, farms, and roads will be placed on the tagboard by taping their tabs to the tagboard.*

Each person in the group will be in charge of six cutout people and one job. All six cutout people will be doing the same job. There are four jobs to choose from: farmer, road builder, house builder, and defender. Your group will decide how many people should be doing each job. Since buildings are worth ten points each, your group may decide to put all of its people to work building houses or they may decide to put the same number of people on each job. It is up to your group to decide.

NOTE: If the group agrees, people can be reassigned to different jobs at any time.

This is how the game is played: If your people are building a house, then you place them where the house is to be placed on the tagboard. If they are farming, then they need to be placed in the farm section. If they are building roads, they need to be placed where the roads will be placed when they are done.

If your townspeople are building houses, you will actually be making the houses for the town. Each house must be colored and cut out. Fold on the dashed lines. The roof must be attached by folding the tabs down and taping it to the top of the house. The house must then be taped to the tagboard.

If your people are building roads, you will be cutting out road sections and taping them to the tagboard. Each rectangle in each section of road must be colored a different color (two adjoining rectangles should not be the same color) Road sections must be colored before they're attached to the tagboard.

If your people are defenders, they are placed along the outside of the tagboard. Defenders do not build anything. Defenders do not earn points while they are defending.

If your people are farming, they need to color each crop, cut the crops out, and then tape them to the tagboard.

At the top of the worksheet titled Hometown, you will see a place to write down the number of people who will do each job in your group. Take a few minutes to talk to the other members of your group and decide how many people will be assigned to each job. Decide which job each person in the group will do.

Give students time to do this.

Any questions? Ready? Begin!

As students progress in making their communities, make "raids" on them by taking houses, plants, and road pieces. As you raid, tell students how easy it was to steal from them because there were no defenses. If students don't figure out a way to defend the community, tell them specifically why it was so easy to raid the community—There was no army protecting your community or There was no wall around your community.

Step Two: Guided Practice

When the time is up, discuss the advantage of having a government that ensures the community's safety. Guide students through the questions in Part II of the Hometown worksheet.

Step Three: Independent Practice

Students will complete the Government Defenses worksheet independently.

Step Four: Closure

Students will write a paragraph telling how they would change the jobs they gave the people of Hometown and why.

The King's House

Name _____

1. Draw the house that was made by your class.

2. What is wrong with the house? _____

3. How could the building process be changed so that the final results would be improved?

    _____

    _____

    _____

4. What is the word that describes a person or group of people who leads other people?

    _____

5. Draw the second house.

6. How is it different from the first house? _____

    _____

    _____

7. As an archaeologist, describe a long street built by a civilization with a government.

    _____

    _____

    _____

8. Describe a long street built by a group of people with no government. _____

    _____

    _____

Building Directions

Government Script: "I am the government. Here are your building instructions."

Group 1—Draw a white rectangle 8" long by 3" tall. Cut out the rectangle. Draw a door 3" from the left side of the rectangle. The door should be 2" tall and 1 1/2" wide. Color it red. Draw black horizontal lines across the remaining white space. The lines should be 1/2" apart.

Group 2—Draw a white rectangle 8" long by 3" high. Draw a 1" square window 2" from each end of the rectangle. Draw 1/4" wide green shutters on both sides of both windows. Draw horizontal black lines across the remaining space. The lines should be 1/2" apart. Cut out the rectangle.

Group 3—Draw a white rectangle 8" long by 3" high. Draw a 1" square window 2" from each end of the rectangle. Draw 1/4" green shutters on both sides of both windows. Draw horizontal black lines across the remaining space. The lines should be 1/2" apart. Cut out the rectangle.

Group 4—Draw a white rectangle 8" long by 3" high. Draw a 1" square window 2" from each end of the rectangle. Draw 1/4" green shutters on both sides of both windows. Draw horizontal black lines across the remaining space. The lines should be 1/2" apart. Cut out the rectangle.

Group 5—Draw a white rectangle 8" long by 3" high. Draw a 1" square window 2" from each end of the rectangle. Draw 1/4" green shutters on both sides of both windows. Draw horizontal black lines across the remaining space. Cut out the rectangle.

Group 6—Draw a white rectangle 8" long by 3" high. Draw a 1" square window 2" from each end of the rectangle. Draw 1/4" green shutters on both sides of both windows. Draw horizontal black lines across the remaining space. The lines should be 1/2" apart. Cut out the rectangle.

Group 7—Draw a white rectangle 8" long by 3" high. Draw a 1" square window 2" from each end of the rectangle. Draw 1/4" green shutters on both sides of both windows. Draw horizontal black lines across the remaining space. The lines should be 1/2" apart. Cut out the rectangle.

Group 8—Draw a white rectangle 8" long by 3" high. Draw a 1" square window 2" from each end of the rectangle. Draw 1/4" green shutters on both sides of both windows. Draw horizontal black lines across the remaining space. The lines should be 1/2" apart. Cut out the rectangle.

Group 9—Draw a rectangle 10" long by 8" wide. Color it red. With black, draw small tiles on it. Cut out the rectangle. Fold it in the middle by making the two 10" sides touch.

Government Projects

Name _____

A. _____   B. _____

1. What are the differences between a project that is done by a government and a project that is done by individuals? _____

_____

_____

2. Why couldn't the system in box B be completed by an individual? _____

_____

C.   *without a government*   D.   *with a government*

3. Why would the system in box D have to be built with the aid of a government? _____

_____

4. What artifacts might an archaeologist find in box C to show that the people had a message system but no government? _____

_____

5. What artifacts might an archaeologist find in box D to show that the people had a message system organized by a government? _____

_____

Hometown

Name _____

Part I

The members of our group have decided to divide up the work in the way shown below.

Farmers _____   Road Builders _____

House Builders _____   Defenders _____

Part II

1. What changes (if any) did you make to the number of people you assigned to each job?

_____

_____

_____

2. Why did you change? _____

_____

3. What were the advantages of changing? _____

_____

4. What were the disadvantages of changing? _____

_____

_____

5. What important factor does a civilization need in order to survive and grow (according to what you have learned from this activity)? _____

_____

_____

6. How would you meet this need? _____

_____

_____

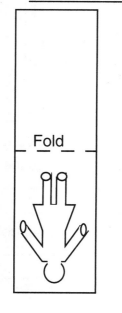 Fold
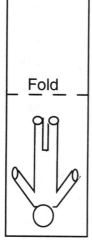 Fold
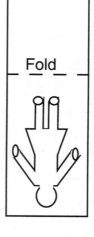 Fold
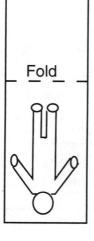 Fold
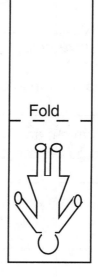 Fold
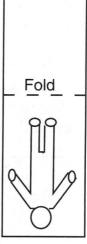 Fold

Houses and Roads

Directions: Color and cut out the objects. Fold on all dashed lines. Glue the roofs to the tops of the houses.

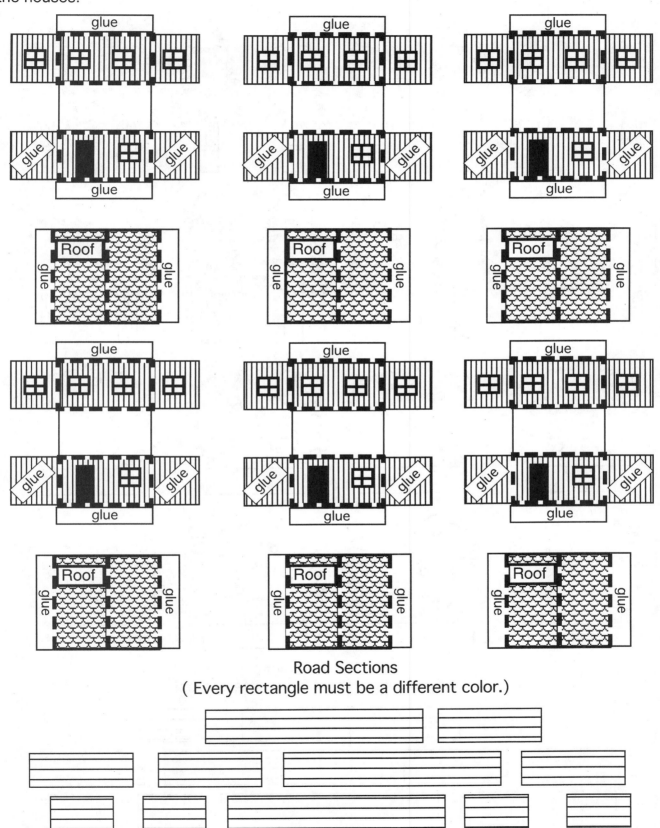

Road Sections
(Every rectangle must be a different color.)

Crops and Roads

Directions: Color and cut out the objects.

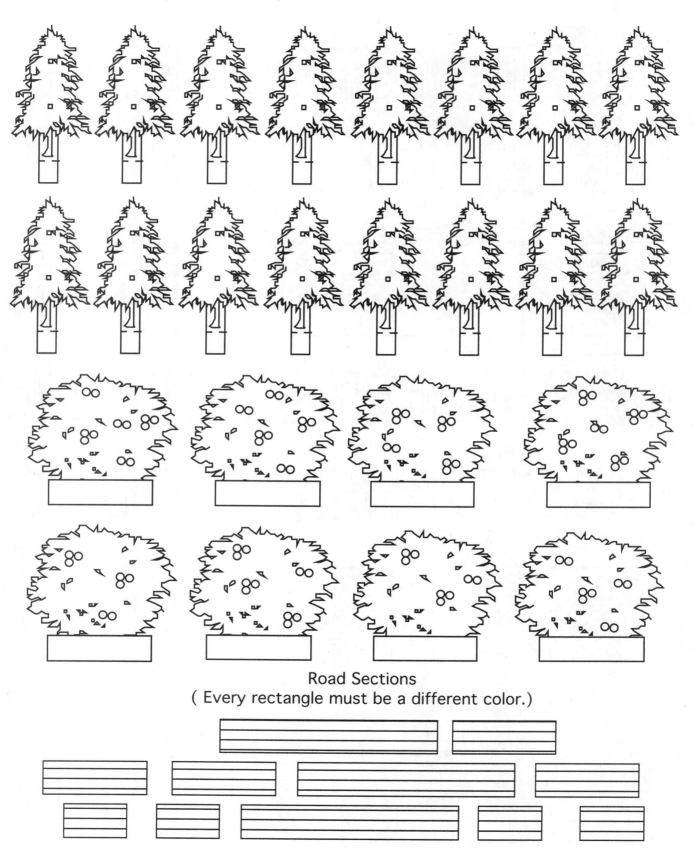

Road Sections
(Every rectangle must be a different color.)

Government Defenses

Name _____

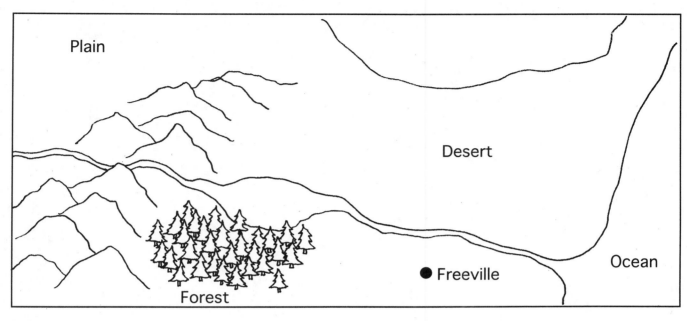

Part I

On the map above, choose the ideal location to start your civilization by drawing a circle around the area and shading the area red. Your circle should be no larger than 1/4 inch across. Explain your decision. Give at least five reasons why you chose the location. _____

_____

_____

_____

_____

_____

Part II

In the space below, draw two artifacts that could be found in an archaeological dig that might tell an archaeologist that a government had created some defense mechanisms. Describe each object.

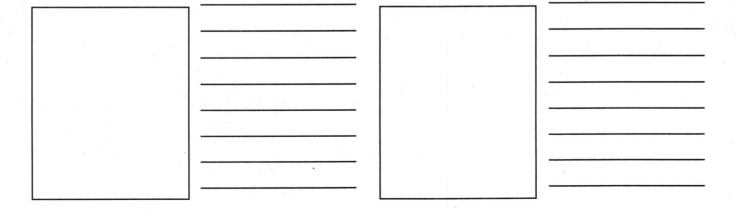

UNIT 5
ARCHAEOLOGICAL DATING METHODS

Chapter 1
Radiocarbon Dating

Background Information

Radiocarbon dating (sometimes called carbon-14 dating) is the most scientifically complex dating method. It is used to date objects that were once alive.

Radiocarbon, or carbon 14, is a radioactive form of carbon. Radiocarbon is formed when cosmic rays enter the upper atmosphere and collide with different kinds of atoms (neutrons, protons, mesons, and other particles) in the air. When neutrons strike nitrogen atoms, the nitrogen atom disintegrates and gives off a proton (nitrogen atoms normally have 14 protons and 14 electrons). When this happens, the nitrogen becomes a radioactive form of carbon called carbon 14. These carbon-14 atoms join oxygen atoms to form a special kind of carbon dioxide ($^{14}CO_2$). This carbon dioxide containing radiocarbon (carbon 14) is swiftly and continuously blown down to the surface of the earth by the planet's constant winds.

A large amount of the radiocarbon is absorbed into the oceans. The remainder is absorbed by plants and animals (humans included). Animals absorb radiocarbon through the air and by eating other plants and animals with radiocarbon. Plants absorb radiocarbon through the air. As long as plants and animals are alive, the level of radiocarbon in their tissues is constantly renewed by feeding and absorption via the air.

Once the plant or animal dies, the radiocarbon within its body decays at an exact and uniform rate into nitrogen—incoming radiocarbon is no longer absorbed. By knowing the rate at which radiocarbon decays into nitrogen, archaeologists can subtract the amount of radiocarbon found in the once-living thing from the known level of carbon 14 and tell how old something is.

Radiocarbon dating is not 100% accurate. It can-

not tell the exact year that something died, but it is accurate to within a few hundred years. Radiocarbon is half gone in about 5700 years. After another 5700 years, half of that amount is gone, and so on. Therefore, it has a half-life of 5700 years. For this reason, radiocarbon dating is not used on objects less than 1,000 years old or more than 50,000 years old. There are additional factors that can cause the dates to be inaccurate, but in the interest of keeping this simple, they will not be discussed in this book.

Lesson 1—Radiocarbon Cycle Diagram

Objective

Students will explain and diagram the steps of the radiocarbon cycle.

Materials

Make a transparency of Radiocarbon Cycle Diagram worksheet • overhead projector • Radiocarbon Cycle Diagram worksheet (one per student) • Your Radiocarbon Cycle Diagram worksheet (2 copies per student) • artifact made of plant or animal material (rag rug, grass basket, wooden candlestick, animal skull, or similar item) or picture of artifact made of plant or animal material

Critical Thinking Skills

- Evaluation
- Application
- Synthesis
- Analysis

Step One: Introducing the Lesson

Show students the artifact made of plant or animal material. Ask students to make guesses about the age of the artifact or object. After each guess, ask students why they made that guess. After a few guesses, ask students if they know a way to tell exactly how old it is. Accept any possibilities. Tell students that they are going to spend the next few lessons learning how archaeologists tell how old things are.

Step Two: Acquiring Information

Distribute the Radiocarbon Cycle Diagram worksheet. Explain to students that they will use this page to take notes. Set up the overhead transparency of the Radiocarbon Cycle Diagram page so you can write notes with the students as the lesson proceeds.

TEACHER SCRIPT: Today, we are going to learn about radiocarbon dating. It is one of the methods that archaeologists use to tell how old something is.

Radiocarbon starts high up in the sky at the top of the atmosphere. Strong energy from space (cosmic rays) soaks this part of the atmosphere. Look at the picture of Earth. Label the upper atmosphere and the cosmic radiation hitting Earth. Write what is happening in Box 1. (Answer: Cosmic radiation hits the Earth.)

In the upper atmosphere, there are a lot of atoms and molecules floating around, just like there are a lot of atoms and molecules floating around us right now. The atoms and molecules make up the air that we breathe. Some of the atoms in the upper atmosphere are nitrogen atoms. Nitrogen atoms have fourteen protons. When a nitrogen atom is struck by cosmic rays from the sun, it loses a proton and changes into a carbon atom that is radioactive. Label the radioactive carbon atom. This is called radiocarbon or carbon-14. Write what is happening in Box 2. (Answer: A nitrogen atom is turned into radiocarbon.)

Carbon-14 atoms join up with oxygen atoms to form a special kind of carbon dioxide ($^{14}CO_2$). Label the radiocarbon atom, the oxygen atoms, and the carbon dioxide. Write what is happening in Box 3. (Answer: Radiocarbon joins with oxygen to form a special kind of carbon dioxide.)

The carbon dioxide containing radiocarbon (carbon-14) is swiftly and continuously blown down to the surface of the earth by the planet's constant winds. Label the wind. A lot of the carbon dioxide goes into the oceans. Label the ocean. The rest is breathed in by plants. Label the plants. Write what is happening in Box 4. (Plants breathe in radiocarbon.)

The plants are then eaten by animals and the ra-diocarbon is passed on to the animal's body. Label the plants with radiocarbon and label the animals. Write what is happening in Box 5. (Answer: Animals take in radiocarbon through the plants they eat.)

Sometimes the animals are eaten by humans. Label the meat with radiocarbon and label the human. The radiocarbon from that animal is then passed on to humans. Write what is happening in Box 6. (Answer: Humans take in radiocarbon by eating animal meat containing radiocarbon.)

As long as plants and animals are alive, they retain a constant level of radiocarbon. Label radiocarbon being eaten. After a long time, radiocarbons turn back into nitrogen again. Label radiocarbon turning into nitrogen. The amount of radiocarbon that turns back into nitrogen is equal to the amount the plant or animal gets from eating. That means that as long as a plant or animal is alive, the amount of radiocarbon stays about the same. Write what is happening in Box 7. (Answer: The number of radiocarbon atoms stays about the same while the body is alive.)

When a plant or animal dies, the radiocarbon in its body keeps turning into nitrogen, but there is no new radiocarbon going in. Label the radiocarbon turning into nitrogen. Write what is happening in Box 8. (Answer: When a body dies, the radiocarbon in the body keeps turning into nitrogen, but no new radiocarbon is taken in.)

All living things have approximately the same amount of radiocarbon in them while they are alive. Because radiocarbon leaves all bodies at the same rate, archaeologists can measure the amount of ra-diocarbon left in a once-living thing and know how long it has been dead. Write what is happening in Box 9. (Answer: Subtract the level of radiocarbon when archaeologists uncover a once-living thing from the level of radiocarbon present in a living thing.)

Radiocarbon dating cannot tell the exact year that something died, but it will tell the age of an object to within a few hundred years. It is not used on objects less than 1000 years old or more than 50,000 years old.

Step Three: Guided Practice

Organize students into groups of five or fewer.

Distribute the Your Radiocarbon Cycle Diagram worksheet (one per student). Ask students to place their Radiocarbon Cycle Diagrams on their desks to use as a reference. Explain to students that they are archaeologists who have just uncovered a shoelace made from cow leather. Students will work together to draw a diagram of one possible life cycle of a radiocarbon atom which could be found in the shoelace. Their diagrams should begin when a nitrogen atom is turned into a radiocarbon atom and should end when the archaeologist uncovers the shoelace and determines its age.

Step Four: Independent Practice

Distribute a second copy of the Your Radiocarbon Cycle Diagram worksheet to each student. Assign one of the following objects to each student in the group: grass basket, wolf skin rug, wig made of real hair, digging stick, mummy, cotton dress, fish head trophy, tepee, ivory statue, a guitar with strings made from cat gut. No two students in the same group should have the same artifact. Students will draw a diagram of one possible life cycle of a radiocarbon atom which could be found in their artifact. Each step should be carefully labeled. The final step will always occur when the archaeologist uncovers the object. The completed worksheet should closely resemble the Radiocarbon Cycle Diagram. Students may ask other students in their group for assistance if they need help. When the students are finished, they should explain their diagrams to the other members of their group.

Lesson 2—Understanding Radiocarbon Decay

Objective

Students will demonstrate an understanding of the process of radiocarbon decay by evaluating analogies between radiocarbon decay and everyday objects.

Materials

Make a transparency of Transparency—Radiocarbon Decay • overhead projector • Radiocarbon Decay worksheet (two copies per student) • Radiocarbon Decay Story Evaluation and writing paper (one of each for each student)

Critical Thinking Skills

• Synthesis

• Application

• Evaluation

Step One: Introducing the Lesson

Begin this lesson with a game called Radiocarbon Decay. This activity requires an open space like the playground or cafeteria. See diagram below.

1. Take approximately one-third of the students and ask them to join hands to form a circle. Explain that they (P's) are going to be a cotton plant for this demonstration. (You may choose any local plant.)

2. Place a second, smaller group of students inside the first, standing individually in a random pattern. (In a class of thirty students, this group should have about six members.) Explain to these students that they are radiocarbon atoms (R).

3. Line up the remaining students one behind the other, facing the circle. Explain to students that they are radiocarbon atoms that the plant is going to breathe in.

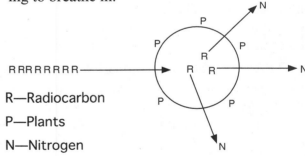

R—Radiocarbon

P—Plants

N—Nitrogen

4. Ask the "plant" students to "breathe in" by raising their arms.

5. Tell three of the "radiocarbon" students to enter the circle.

6. Tell three of the "radiocarbon" students that were in the circle at the beginning to exit the circle in the opposite direction and become "nitrogen atoms." Point out that the number of "radiocarbon atoms" remains about the same.

7. Repeat the process two or three times, explaining each time what is happening. By the third time, students should be able to tell the steps themselves.

8. Next, ask students what would happen if the plant died. Using students as part of the demonstration, students inside the circle ("radiocarbons") should join the "nitrogen atoms" one or two at a time at ten to twenty second intervals until there are no "radiocarbon" students left in the circle.

9. Regroup the students and repeat the scenario. Allow students as a group to explain what is happening. This time, stop the process after the plant has died, but before all of the "radiocarbon atoms" have turned into "nitrogen atoms." Ask the students to figure out how the archaeologist would tell how old the plant was. (Subtract the number of "radiocarbon atoms" they finished with from the original number in the circle. In order to figure out an age, students need to know a rate of decay, which you can randomly fix at one atom every 100 years. Students then multiply their answer times 100.)

10. Students write a paragraph comparing the game to radiocarbon decay.

Step Two: Guided Practice

Display Transparency—Radiocarbon Decay on the overhead projector. Cover all squares except Square 1 with a piece of paper. Uncover the remaining squares as they are discussed in the script below.

TEACHER SCRIPT: (Square 1) *What will happen to a string of Christmas tree lights if someone plugs them in and never unplugs them?* (Eventually, they will start to burn out.) *Will all the lights burn out at one time?* (No, they will probably burn out one or two at a time.) (Square 2)

Suppose that every time a bulb burns out, someone immediately replaces the burned-out bulb with a new one. If a red one burns out, they immediately put another red one in and so on. What will happen to the number of lights? (It will stay the same.) (Square 3) *Does this remind you of something you just did?* (The radiocarbon game)

What will happen to the string of lights if they are left plugged in and no one replaces the lights as they burn out? (Square 4, Square 5) (Eventually they will all burn out.) (Square 6)

In this story, I compared a string of Christmas tree lights to radiocarbon atoms. When we use a story like this to compare two things that are not alike, it *is called an analogy. Now, you are going to work together to write your own analogy about radiocarbon decay.*

Divide students into small groups. Distribute Radiocarbon Decay worksheet (one copy per student). Tell them that they are going to work together to make an analogy about radiocarbon decay. Tell students that gasoline will represent radiocarbon atoms. Students will illustrate and explain each step on the Radiocarbon Decay worksheet. Assist each group as needed. If a group gets stalled, remind them of how gas is used to run a car. Ask them what happens when the gas runs out.

Step Three: Independent Practice

Distribute a second copy of the Radiocarbon Decay worksheet. Each group will now come up with their own analogy to radiocarbon decay. If the groups get stalled in coming up with ideas, suggest that they make a list of things that are always running out of fuel or energy, like batteries or gasoline (portable radios in their hometown, flashlights in their house, the light bulbs in their house, the lawn mowers on their street, the street lamps in their town, etc.).

Once the group has come up with an idea, students will complete the page independently.

Lesson 3—Radiocarbon Dating

Objective

Students will choose which objects can be dated using the radiocarbon dating method and explain why they made their choice.

Materials

Make a transparency of Transparency—Radiocarbon Dating • Radiocarbon Dating—Artifacts worksheet (one per student)

Critical Thinking Skills

• Synthesis

• Analysis

Step One: Introducing the Lesson

TEACHER SCRIPT: *Today we are going to apply what we have learned about radiocarbon dating to artifacts found at an archaeological site.*

Step Two: Guided Practice

Place Transparency—Radiocarbon Dating on the overhead projector. Ask students to review the types of artifacts that can be dated using radiocarbon dating. (They must be made from materials that were once alive. They must be between 1000 and 50,000 years old.) Point to the first artifact. Ask students if the radiocarbon dating method can be used to date that artifact. Ask them to explain their answers. Repeat this process for the rest of the artifacts. (See answers in back of book.)

Step Three: Independent Practice

Distribute Radiocarbon Dating—Artifacts worksheet. Students will follow the directions printed at the top of the sheet. They will place an X next to items on which an archaeologist could use radiocarbon dating. At the bottom of the page, students will explain why they could not use the radiocarbon dating method on the items they did not check.

Lesson 4—Counting the Years

Objective

Students will figure out the age of an object from the number of radiocarbon atoms remaining in it.

Materials

Counting the Years worksheet (one copy per student)

Critical Thinking Skills

• Application

• Synthesis

Step One: Introducing the Lesson

TEACHER SCRIPT: *Today we are going to use the radiocarbon dating method to figure out the ages of some artifacts.*

Step Two: Guided Practice

This lesson will show students how the dating process works. These numbers are highly simplified so students can easily work with them and still understand the concept of radiocarbon dating.

For the purposes of this lesson, we will assume every living thing has 22,136 carbon-14 atoms. We will also assume that when a living thing dies, the carbon 14 decays at a rate of 2 atoms per year.

Distribute the Counting the Years worksheet. Work through the example and the first problem with students until they understand how to work these problems.

Step Three: Independent Practice

Students will complete the remainder of the Counting the Years worksheet independently.

Step Four: Closure

Draw a simple wooden door on the blackboard. Tell students that it has been uncovered in an archaeological dig. Ask students to figure out its age if it contains 518 atoms. Tell students to assume every living thing contains 22,136 carbon-14 atoms and that when a living thing dies, the carbon 14 decays at a rate of 2 atoms per year.

CLOSURE ANSWER: $(22{,}136 - 518)/2 = 10{,}809$ years old

Radiocarbon Cycle Diagram

Name _____

	1
	2
C-14 + O / O → C-14 O / O	3
	4
	5
	6
	7
	8
	9

Your Radiocarbon Cycle Diagram

Name _____

Item _____

	1
	2
	3
	4
	5
	6
	7
	8
	9

Transparency—Radiocarbon Decay

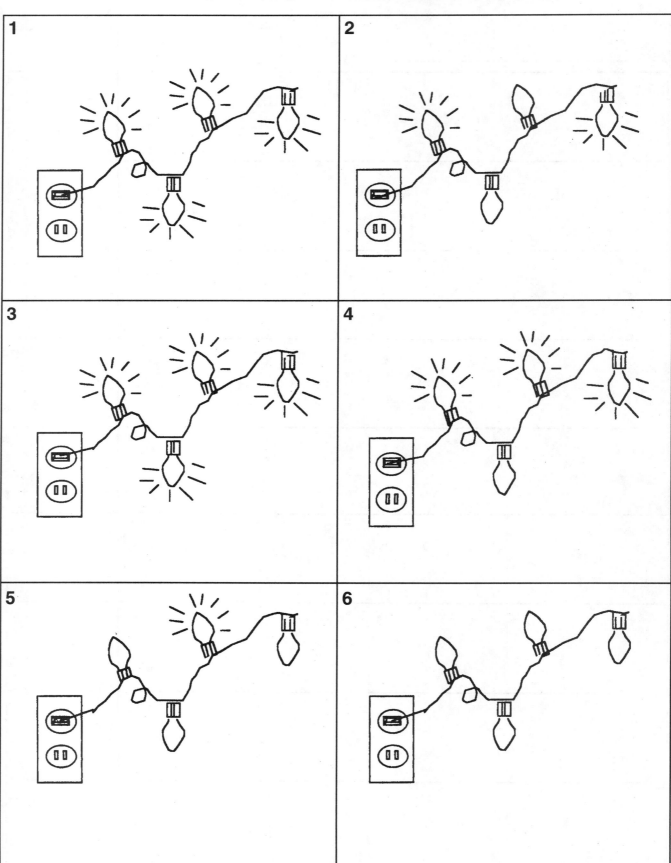

Radiocarbon Decay

Name _____

1	**2**
3	**4**
5	**6**
7	**8**

Transparency—Radiocarbon Dating

1

computer manufactured in 1985 A.D.

2

wood clock manufactured in 1800 A.D.

3

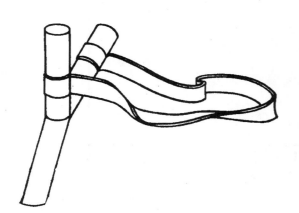

leather sling on slingshot made in 500 A.D.

4

plastic toothbrush manufactured in 1900 A.D.

5

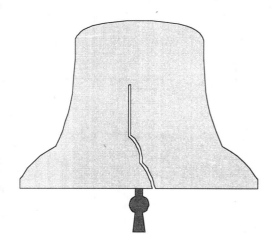

metal bell manufactured in 1776 A.D.

6

wooden spool of cotton thread made in 200 B.C.

Radiocarbon Dating—Artifacts

Name _____

Part I

Directions: Place an X next to those items on which an archaeologist could use radiocarbon dating.

1. _____ dinosaur bones
2. _____ a wooden chair
3. _____ wool cloth
4. _____ a fallen tree
5. _____ a living tree
6. _____ glass vase

8. _____ a copper spoon
9. _____ stone arrowheads
10. _____ a book published in 1994
11. _____ sheep bones
12. _____ cotton carrying bag
13. _____ caveman's digging stick

Part II

Directions: On the lines below, list each object from the list above that you DID NOT mark with an X. For each object, explain why you do not think that an archaeologist could use radiocarbon dating to determine its age. Be sure to start a new paragraph for each object. Start your paragraph by giving the name and number of the object from the list above.

_____

_____

_____

_____

_____

_____

_____

_____

_____

_____

_____

_____

_____

_____

Counting the Years

Name _____

For this lesson, we are going to pretend that every living thing contains 22,136 carbon-14 atoms. When each thing dies, we will pretend that the carbon-14 will decay at a rate of 2 atoms per year.

Example: An archaeologist uncovers a grass basket. He uses radiocarbon testing to determine the basket's age. The test shows that there are 17,666 carbon-14 atoms remaining in the grass. This means that 4,470 carbon-14 atoms have turned back into nitrogen since the grasses died. If Carbon-14 decays at a rate of 2 atoms per year, dividing 4,470 by 2 will give us the number of years since the grass died. 4,470 divided by 2 gives 2,235 years. The archaeologist can then conclude that the basket was made 2,235 years ago.

1. A cotton carrying bag contains 6,392 carbon-14 atoms. How old is the bag? _____

  22,136 – 6392= _____ Divide this answer by 2 to get your answer.

2. A piece of wool cloth contains 4,508 carbon-14 atoms. How old is the cloth? _____

3. Sheep bones contain 10,740 carbon-14 atoms. How old are the sheep bones? _____

4. A wooden chair contains 3,012 carbon-14 atoms. How old is the wooden chair? _____

5. Chinese rice paper contains 1,556 carbon-14 atom. How old is the paper? _____

6. Paint made from cow's blood contains 9,996 carbon-14 atoms. How old is the paint? _____

Chapter 2
Tree Ring Dating

Background Information

Tree ring dating (dendrochronology) is the science of dating past events and artifacts by studying the successive annual growth rings within a tree. Every year, a living tree will grow a new ring. By looking at a tree stump, the trunk of a tree that has been cut down, or a "core sample," one can see concentric rings that get smaller the closer you get to the center of the tree's trunk. (A core sample is a sample taken from the inside of a living tree. A small tool is used to extract a 4 mm. core in diameter. The core sample can have varying lengths and does not harm the tree.) The amount of space between the rings can vary from year to year. In years with heavy rainfall, the tree grows a lot and there is a larger space between the rings. In years when there is less rainfall, the space is smaller. Because of the fluctuating level of rain, there is an obvious, unique pattern in the rings.

Weather and climate vary from place to place; therefore, trees that grow in the same area have a similar pattern. If archaeologists are going to date an artifact using tree ring dating, they must know the area the artifact came from. They must also have a known sample of a tree from that area. By counting the rings of the known sample and then comparing that sample to the artifact, archaeologists are able to obtain an accurate age of the artifact.

Lesson 1—Counting Tree Rings

Objective

Given the cross-section of a tree and the year it was cut, students will count the number of rings in a given sample and determine the years in which the various rings were formed.

Materials

Tree Rings Part I worksheet, Tree Rings Part II worksheet (one copy of each per student) • cross-section of a real tree branch, log, or old stump

Critical Thinking Skills

• Application

• Analysis

Step One: Introducing the Lesson

Tell students they are going to study a second method of dating artifacts called tree ring dating. Show students a piece of wood with visible rings—a log or an old stump will work. Explain that during each year of the tree's life, a ring of new growth grows just under the bark. This growth makes the tree wider. Ask them to look at the rings closely. Ask them if all the rings are the same size. Ask them to make guesses as to why the rings might be different sizes. If they don't guess, tell them that during years with a lot of rain, the tree will grow a lot, and the rings will be farther apart. During years with little rain, the tree will grow only a little, and the rings will be closer together. Talk about conditions that could make the tree grow a lot or a little during a particular year. Ask students to make a guess about all the other trees that grew next to this one. (Their tree ring pattern should be similar.) If someone cuts down a tree and makes a piece of furniture, like a table, you can see the rings in the furniture. If you compare the ring pattern in the table to the ring pattern in a tree from the same area, you can tell when the table was made.

Step Two: Guided Practice

Distribute the Tree Rings Part I worksheet. Ask students to look at the cross-section of the tree shown at the top of the Tree Rings Part I worksheet. Ask them to put their finger on the last ring the tree grew. Check to make sure all students have their finger on the outermost ring. Ask them to remove their fingers. Read the first sentence on the page, *"This tree was cut down in 1965."* Ask students to point to the ring that was grown in 1965. Again, they should have pointed to the outermost ring. If they count backwards to the innermost ring, they will know the year the tree began to grow. Complete the questions in section A with students.

Read the paragraph on core samples below section A. Ask students to look at core sample B. Ask them to point to the outer ring of the core sample under the bark. Check to make sure that students are pointing to the line on the far left side of the core sample. Ask them to count the spaces backwards from the left line until they get to the line on the far right side of the core sample. Then they will know the year the tree began to grow. Check to make sure students understand. Students subtract their answer from the year the core sample was taken to find out how old the tree was at that time. Repeat this process with core sample C.

Students will then cut out the core sample at the bottom of the page and match it to the tree cross-section shown in D. Students then count backwards along the core sample from 1968 until they get to the outside ring of the tree. That is the year the tree was cut. They should then count backwards to the innermost ring to find out when the tree began to grow.

Step Three: Independent Practice

Students will complete the Tree Rings Part II worksheet independently.

Lesson 2—Tree Ring Dating

Objective

Students will be able to "date" a "wooden artifact" by using a simulated core sample.

Materials

Tree Ring Dating worksheet (one copy per student)

Critical Thinking Skills

- Analysis
- Synthesis

Step One: Introducing the Lesson

Distribute copies of the Tree Ring Dating worksheet. Ask students to look at the core sample at the bottom of the page. It was taken in 1993. Ask them to point to the line that indicates 1993 (the outermost line under the bark). Ask them how they might figure out how old the Chair Leg is. (They will need to compare the rings of the core sample to the rings of the chair leg.)

Step Two: Guided Practice

Students will cut out the core sample at the bottom of the Tree Ring Dating worksheet, and try to line up the ring patterns with those of the first furniture sample. The edge of the core sample should be lined up so that it will pass though the center of the ring pattern. Students will be able to tell when the furniture was made by counting backward from 1993 on the core sample until they reach the outer ring of the furniture sample. Check answers, and reteach as needed.

Step Three: Independent Practice

Students will complete the remainder of the activities independently.

Lesson 3—Dating Artifacts

Objective

Students will be able to indicate which artifacts could be dated using the tree ring dating method.

Critical Thinking Skills

- Analysis

Materials

Artifacts—Tree Ring Dating worksheet (one per student) • overhead projector

Step One: Introducing the Lesson

Ask students if they know what kind of artifacts can be dated using the tree ring dating method. List their answers on the chalkboard. If students have not suggested the following items, add them to the list on the chalkboard: 1) The artifacts must be made of wood. 2) The archaeologist must be able to see the rings of the wood in the object. 3) The objects must not be older than about 8,000 years because there are no core samples that are that old.

Step Two: Guided Practice

Find six artifacts—three that can be dated using the tree ring dating method and three that cannot. Divide students into small groups. Show the artifacts one at a time and ask them to decide as a group whether it could be dated using the tree ring dating method. If their answer is no, ask them to decide why not. Discuss answers as a class (Possible artifacts: wood desk, book, ceramic coffee cup, wooden door, wood picture frame, handwritten letter, computer disk, shirt, wooden spoon or spoon handle)

Step Three: Independent Practice

Distribute Artifacts—Tree Ring Dating worksheet. Students will place an X next to those items which could be dated using tree ring dating. At the bottom of the page, students will explain why they could not use tree ring dating on those artifacts they did not check.

Tree Rings Part I

Name _____

A. This tree was cut down in 1965.

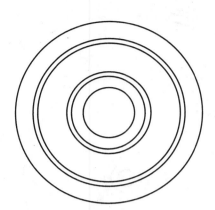

1. When did this tree begin to grow?
    _____

2. How old was this tree when it was cut down? _____

3. Which year had the most rain?
    _____

4. Which years had very little rain?
    _____

The tool shown in the box to the right is a special kind of saw that an archaeologist can use to take a round sample from a living tree. It does not hurt the tree. The sample looks like the strips below, showing all the rings as stripes. The strips below are called "core samples."

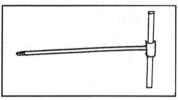

B. This core sample was cut in 1995.

1. What year did this tree begin to grow? _____

2. How old was this tree when the core sample was taken? _____

C. This core sample was cut in 1934.

1. What year did this tree begin to grow? _____

2. How old was this tree when the core sample was taken? _____

D. Cut off the core sample on the bottom of this page. It was taken in 1968 from a tree near the one shown on the left. Match the core sample to the cross-section of the tree on the left.

1. When was the tree cut?_____

2. When did this tree begin to grow? _____

3. How old was this tree when it was cut down? _____

4. Which year had the least rain?
    _____

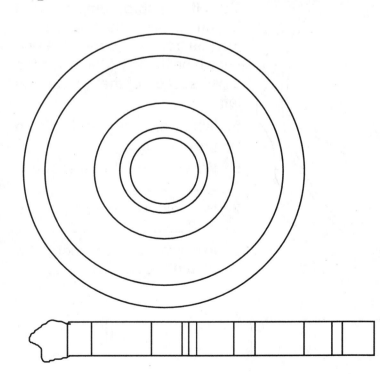

Tree Rings Part II

Name _____

This tree was cut down in 1982.

1. When did this tree begin to grow? _____

2. How old was this tree when it was cut down? _____

3. Which years had the most rain? _____

4. Which years had very little rain? _____

Cut off the core sample at the bottom of this page. It was taken in 1959 from a tree near the one shown on the left. Match it to the cross-section of the tree on the left.

5. When did the tree begin to grow? _____

6. When was the tree cut? _____

7. How old was it when it was cut? _____

8. In which years was there a lot of rain? _____

Tree Ring Dating

Name _____

Directions: Cut out the core sample at the bottom of the page. The core sample was taken in 1993. Compare the ring pattern of the core sample to the ring pattern of the furniture samples on this page. Determine the age of each piece of furniture and when it was made. (Remember that if the furniture is made of more than one piece of wood, the most recent ring will show when the tree was cut. Assume the furniture was made in the year the tree was cut.)

Chair Leg

In what year was it made? _____

How old is this chair? _____

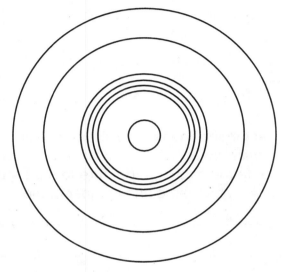

Door Jamb

In what year was it made? _____

How old is this door jamb? _____

Picture Frame

In what year was it made? _____

How old is this picture frame? _____

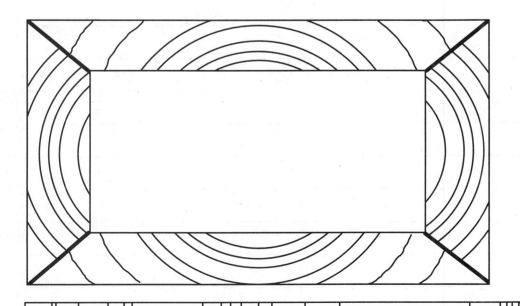

(core sample taken in 1993)

Artifacts—Tree Ring Dating

Name _____

Part I

Directions: Place an X next to those items on which an archaeologist could use tree ring dating.

1. _____ a book published in 1840

2. _____ glass vase

3. _____ Civil War wooden gun stock

4. _____ dinosaur bones

5. _____ caveperson's digging stick

6. _____ cotton bag

7. _____ burnt firewood

8. _____ board from a roof rafter

9. _____ fallen tree

10. _____ wooden fence post

Part II

Directions: On the lines below, list each object from the list above that you DID NOT mark with an X. For each object, explain why you do not think that an archaeologist could use tree ring dating to determine its age. Be sure to start a new paragraph for each object. Start your paragraph by giving the name and number of the object from the list above.

_____

_____

_____

_____

_____

_____

_____

_____

_____

_____

_____

_____

_____

_____

_____

_____

Chapter 3
Cultural Dating

Background Information

We have discussed two methods of dating artifacts—radiocarbon dating and tree ring dating. A third method that archaeologists use to date artifacts is called cultural dating. Cultural dating compares styles of pottery, architecture, or metal work with styles from known time periods. In order to use this method, the archaeologist must be familiar with the time period or be willing to research the information that is needed.

Cultural dating is the least scientific of the three methods. There is nothing to measure or count. It is only as accurate as the information that is already known about a given civilization.

Lesson 1—Introduction to Cultural Dating

Objective

Students will use a miniature "library" of information to identify the culture in which an artifact belongs and to determine the approximate age of the artifact.

Materials

An old plastic object (an old doll, a figurine, an old salt shaker, etc.) • American Cultural Dating worksheet and Cultural Dating II worksheet (one copy of each for each student)

Critical Thinking Skills

• Application
• Analysis

Step One: Introducing the Lesson

Show students the old plastic object. Tell them that this artifact was uncovered by an archaeologist. Ask them if the archaeologist can use radiocarbon dating to date the object. (No, the plastic was never alive.) Ask them to explain their answers. Ask them if the archaeologist can use tree ring dating. Ask them to explain why tree ring dating could not be used. (The object is not made of wood.) Tell students that

they will now study the third method that archaeologists use to date artifacts. This method can be used to date artifacts like the plastic object. It is called cultural dating.

Step Two: Guided Practice

Distribute the American Cultural Dating worksheet. Read the introductory material to students. Ask students to look at artifact #1. Talk about its characteristics. Ask students to look in their "library" and find the approximate dates the artifact may have been made. Subtract the approximate date from the current year to find the approximate age. Students will write the age in the space below artifact #1. Check answers before continuing. Repeat the process with artifact #2. Check answers before continuing. Allow students to complete the remainder of the worksheet, giving assistance as needed. Check all answers before continuing.

Step Three: Independent Practice

Distribute Cultural Dating II worksheet. Students identify the characteristics of artifacts 1–6 at the top of the page. They use the "library" at the bottom of the page to identify the culture the artifacts belong to and the approximate date they were created.

Step Four: Closure

Students will look again at the old plastic object that was shown at the beginning of the lesson. Students will write a paragraph explaining the process that they would use to find out what culture the object came from and the approximate age of the object.

Lesson 2—Cultural Dating: Artifacts

Objective

Students will be able to distinguish between objects that could be dated using the cultural dating method and objects that could not. Students will be able to explain their decisions.

Materials

8 pieces of drawing paper (approximately 6" x 8"), Cultural Dating— Artifacts worksheet (one copy per student) • model car or picture of car

Critical Thinking Skills

- Application
- Analysis

Step One: Introducing the Lesson

Divide the students into six or eight groups of no more than four students. Give half of the groups a piece of drawing paper labeled "object that can be dated using cultural dating." Give the other groups a piece of drawing paper labeled "object that cannot be dated using cultural dating." Give each group ten minutes to find an object in the classroom that fits the category written on their paper. Groups will then draw the object on the paper.

At the end of ten minutes, ask each group to show their drawings. Discuss whether each drawing is correct.

Step Two: Guided Practice

Distribute Cultural Dating—Artifacts worksheet. Students will complete Part I of the worksheet by placing an X next to those objects which an archaeologist could date using cultural dating.

When the students have finished, ask students to vote on a dating method for each object by a show of hands. Ask one or two students to defend their choice.

Step Three: Independent Practice

Students will complete Part II of the Cultural Dating—Artifacts worksheet.

Step Four: Closure

Students will look at the model car or the picture of a car. Students will write down why they think that cultural dating should be used to date this object.

CLOSURE ANSWER: Radiocarbon dating cannot be used because the parts of the car are not made of materials that were once alive. Tree ring dating cannot be used because none of the car parts are made of wood.

American Cultural Dating

Name _____

Archaeologists sometimes use a method called cultural dating to date artifacts found in a dig. In order to use this method, the archaeologist looks at the style of the object, the materials it was made from, and how it was made. He then compares this information to what is already known about the culture of the place in which the dig is located. By making comparisons, the archaeologist can determine the approximate age of the artifact.

Directions: At the left, there is a cultural library that you will use to try to determine the approximate years in which the artifacts at the right may have been made. Write the approximate age of the object in the space provided.

LIBRARY

1650–1770

The Puritans of New England wore floor-length skirts and shirts of darker colors. They wore a ruffled white collar and a white cap.

1770–1790

Women wore tight corsets to make their waists look small and hoops to make their skirts very wide. They wore large fancy hats.

1790–1823

Women's dresses had scoop necklines that were low and waistlines that were high. The skirt was straight from the waist to the floor.

1870–1890

Women's dresses were still floor-length. The back of the dress had a bustle (an extra piece of material gathered at the sides).

1900–1920

Women's skirts began to get shorter. For the first time in American history, it was proper for women's legs to be uncovered. By the 1920s, the knees could be seen. The dresses were loose and the waists settled on the hips.

1940–1960

In the 1940s, it became acceptable for women to wear pantsuits. The pants had flared legs. The dresses were knee-length with full skirts.

1. Age _____

2. Age _____

3. Age _____

4. Age _____

5. Age _____

6. Age _____

Cultural Dating II

Name _____

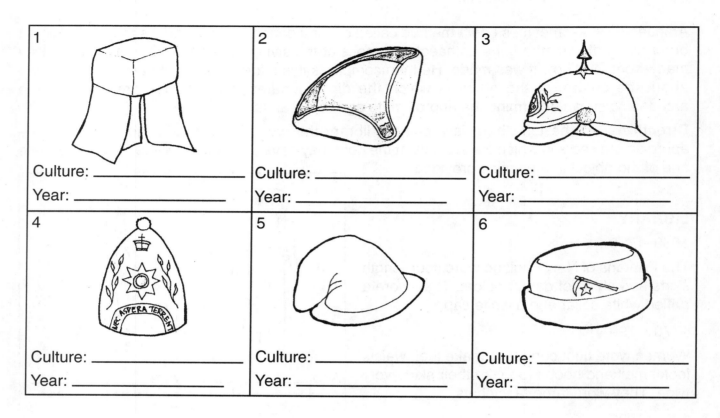

1
Culture: _____
Year: _____

2
Culture: _____
Year: _____

3
Culture: _____
Year: _____

4
Culture: _____
Year: _____

5
Culture: _____
Year: _____

6
Culture: _____
Year: _____

LIBRARY

Russia

1670 A.D. Infantrymen wore cloth hats with rounded peaks that fell slightly backwards.

1700 A.D. Infantrymen wore hats that looked like a box sitting on the head with flaps that went down past the chin.

1882 A.D. Infantrymen wore a round cloth hat that was flat on top. The bottom edge was folded up to form a cuff. There was an insignia on the front.

Germany, Saxony Province

1600 A.D.–1720 A.D. Infantrymen wore black tri-corner hats.

1720 A.D.–1765 A.D. Infantrymen wore tall, pointed caps with a star and crown on the front.

1866 A.D.–1920 A.D. Infantrymen wore hard helmets topped with a sharp spike.

Cultural Dating—Artifacts

Name _____

Part I

Directions: Place an X next to those objects on which an archaeologist could use cultural dating.

1. _____ a carved wooden chair
2. _____ a dinosaur bone
3. _____ a fallen tree
4. _____ human skeleton
5. _____ cotton dress

6. _____ burnt firewood
7. _____ a gun
8 _____ silver candlesticks
9. _____ wooden fence post
10. _____ a wedding ring

Part II

Directions: On the lines below, list each object from the list above that you DID NOT mark with an X. For each object, explain why you think that an archaeologist could not use cultural dating to determine its age. Be sure to start a new paragraph for each object. Start your paragraph by giving the name and number of the object from the list above.

_____

_____

_____

_____

_____

_____

_____

_____

_____

_____

_____

_____

_____

_____

_____

_____

Chapter 4
Dating Methods Review

Lesson 1—Dating Methods Review

Objective

Students will choose one of the three methods used for dating artifacts and justify their answers.

Materials

Writing paper • Dating Artifacts Review worksheet and Dating Methods Review Dig worksheet (one copy for each student) • completed Field Record and Field Square Plan from Unit 1, Chapter 2, Lesson 3 writing paper • wooden walking stick, glass vase, and string

Critical Thinking Skills

- Application
- Analysis
- Synthesis
- Evaluation

Step One: Introducing the Lesson

Distribute writing paper. Write the three methods of dating artifacts on the chalkboard (radiocarbon dating, tree ring dating, and cultural dating). Divide students into pairs. Show students the wooden walking stick, and ask them to draw it at the top of their papers. Working as a pair, students should choose the best dating method. They should write down their choice and their reasons for making that choice. Discuss reasons as a class. Repeat the process with the string and the vase. (See answers in back of book.)

Step Two: Guided Practice

Students will complete Dating Artifacts Review worksheet with their partners. Assist students as necessary.

When students are finished, combine pairs of students to make groups of four. Students will discuss their answers.

Step Three: Independent Practice

Students will look around their homes and bring in two objects that could be dated using radiocarbon dating at some time in the future, two objects that could be dated using tree ring dating, and two objects that could be dated using cultural dating. On notebook paper, students will explain in writing why their artifacts should be dated using the method they chose. Students will then choose one or two of their artifacts to share with the class. After displaying the artifact, the student will ask the class to vote on which dating method they would use. The student will then explain to the class which method he/she thought should be used and why it is the best choice. (If you wish to make this an entirely in-class activity, students may cut their artifacts from mail-order catalogs.)

Step Four: More Independent Practice

Students will design their own dig using the Dating Methods Review Dig worksheet. Students will draw 6 artifacts (or cut out pictures from mail-order catalogs). They will choose two artifacts that can be dated using each dating method. They will number artifacts 1–6. They may place them anywhere on the Field Square Plan at the top of the worksheet.

At the bottom of the paper, students will describe the numbered items and tell which method of dating should be used and why. Pass digs around the class so that each student has the opportunity to view at least four other digs. On a piece of paper, students write down any artifacts they think should be dated differently and explain why. Discuss disagreements as a class.

Step Five: Closure

Display the enlarged Field Square Plans from the Archaeological Digs in Unit One. On notebook paper, ask students to list ten artifacts shown in the Field Square Plans. (You may choose ten specific artifacts, if desired.) Then students will write down which dating method they would use to find the age of each object.

Regroup students as they were grouped while uncovering the archaeological dig. Students will compare their dating method choices and discuss any discrepancies.

Dating Artifacts Review

Name _____

Directions: Write down the dating method you would use to date each of the following artifacts. Explain why you chose the dating method in the Reason column.

ARTIFACT	DATING METHOD	REASON
1 skull bone		
2 leather shoe		
3 clay tablets with story		
4 pottery jar with pictures of an Egyptian king		
5 wooden milking stool		
6 garden hoe made from a sharpened deer antler		
7 sculpture of a horse found next to a book of poetry		
8 wood fence post		
9 cave painting		
10 metal lantern with a candle inside		

Dating Methods Review Dig

Name _____

	A	B	C	D
5				
4				
3				
2				
1				

Artifact #	Dating Method Used	Reason for Choosing this Method
1		
2		
3		
4		
5		
6		

EXTENSION ACTIVITIES

Review of Archaeology

Regular intermittent review is necessary to reinforce concepts that have been taught. Information must be presented many times before students internalize it. The following activities can be added to the study of any civilization.

Activity 1

Ask students to complete a Culture Mind Map. They can find two examples of each of the five aspects for the culture they are currently studying. (page 106)

Activity 2

Students will use the information from the American Culture Mind Map to write a short report explaining how artifacts can give archaeologists clues to American culture.

Activity 3

Ask students to draw and label those things which indicate that the civilization that they are studying had an organized government. They may use the Proof of an Organized Government worksheet provided. (page 107)

Activity 4

Ask students to find two artifacts whose uses are known only because of the locations in which they were found and/or because of the objects that were found in their proximity. Students may use the Artifacts and Location work page. (page 108)

Activity 5

Choose an artifact that is characteristic of the civilization that is being studied. Pictures can be located in textbooks and magazines such as the *National Geographic*. Ask students to complete the Artifact Study worksheet. (page 109)

Activity 6

Provide students with a copy of the Field Square Plan from Unit One, page 22. Ask students to draw an archaeological dig of either a house or a village that is typical of the civilization that is being studied. On a separate piece of paper, students will list each artifact and its coordinates on the Field Square Plan.

Activity 7

Ask students to choose one type of artifact from the culture they are studying. For instance, they might choose architecture, poetry, painting, clothing, religion, etc. Then they should create a time line with pictures showing the change in the artifacts over time.

Activity 8

Ask students to look at artifacts in their textbook, magazines, and reference books. They should place the artifacts into one of three categories: Artifacts that Could be Dated Using the Radiocarbon Dating Method, Artifacts that Could be Dated Using the Tree Ring Dating Method, and Artifacts that Could be Dated Using the Cultural Dating Method.

Culture Mind Map

Name _____

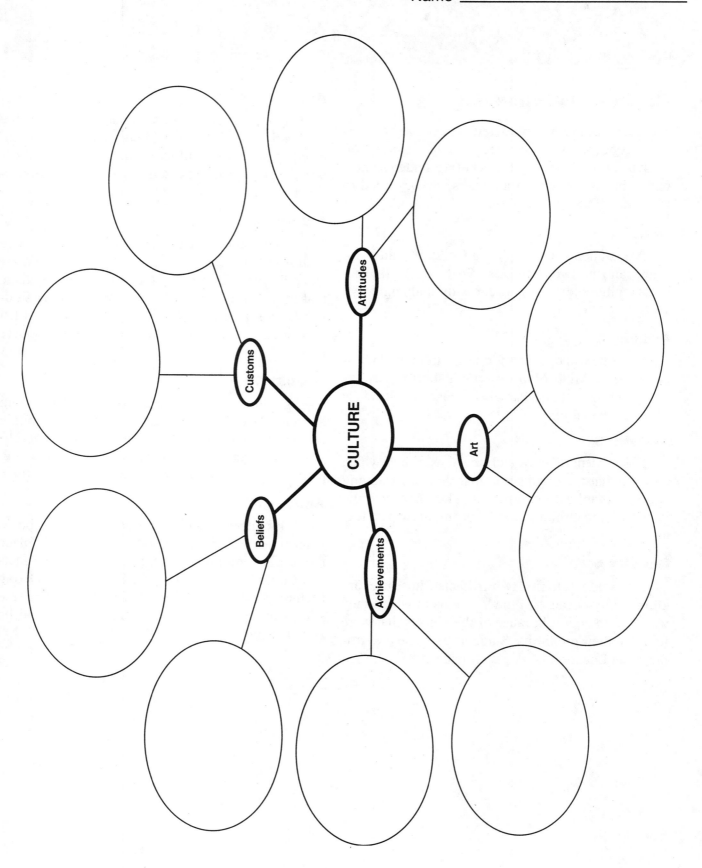

Proof of an Organized Government

Name _____

Directions: Draw and label the items that indicate that the civilization you are studying had an organized government.

1. _____
_____
_____

2. _____
_____
_____

3. _____
_____
_____

4. _____
_____
_____

5. _____
_____
_____

6. _____
_____
_____

Artifacts and Location

Name _____

Directions: In the reference materials that you have available to you, find two artifacts whose uses were determined only by either the location in which they were found or by the other objects that were located near them. Draw and label each artifact. Then answer the questions below.

1. ARTIFACT #1

2. How was this artifact used? _____
_____

3. How did archaeologists know that this is how it was used? _____
_____

4. Suggest another use for this artifact. What clue(s) might have led archaeologists to believe that this was how the artifact was used? _____
_____

5. ARTIFACT #2

6. How was this artifact used? _____
_____

7. How did archaeologists know that this is how it was used? _____
_____

8. Suggest another use for this artifact. What clue(s) might have led archaeologists to believe that this was how the artifact was used? _____
_____

Artifact Study

Name _____

Directions: In the reference materials you have available to you, choose an artifact that is characteristic of the civilization you are studying. Then complete the questions below.

1. Sketch the artifact.

2. What does this artifact tell you about this civilization? _____
_____

   a. Customs? _____
_____

   b. Beliefs? _____
_____

   c. Achievements? _____
_____

   d. Art? _____
_____

   e. Attitudes? _____
_____

3. What is the level of technology of this civilization? _____

   Explain your answer. _____
_____

4. Was this society a hunter-gatherer society or an agricultural-based society? _____

   Explain your answer. _____
_____

5. What dating method would an archaeologist use to determine this artifact's age? _____
_____

   Explain your answer. _____
_____

Answers

Introduction to Strata (p. 4)

1. E

2. A

3. Answers will vary. It will be an object drawn in stratum E.

4. The object in stratum A

5. Answers will vary. It will be the object drawn in stratum A.

   Newest

Deeper is Older (p. 7)

See sample entry on page 3.

Archaeological Record (p. 8)

See sample entry on page 3.

Field Square Plan Practice (p. 13)

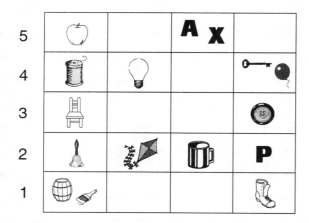

1. C2
2. B4
3. See map
4. See map
5. A3
6. D1
7. A1
8. B2
9. D4
10. A5
11–16. See map

Location, Location, Location! Part I (p. 27)

A. 1. They sat on it while eating meals.

   2. The table, silverware, plates

   3. People did not face each other when they ate. They sat on the couch together.

B. 1. They slept on the couch.

2. The pillow at one end, the sock, the dress on the hanger.

3. They slept alone. The common area also serves as a sleep area.

C. 1. The tire was tied to the rope and it was used as a swing.

   2. The tree limb, the tire

   3. They liked to play. They recycled old things.

D. 1. The rope was used to lower the bucket into the well to get water.

   2. The circle of rocks, the bucket

   3. They knew how to dig a well. They knew how to make a wooden bucket. They didn't have indoor plumbing.

Location, Location, Location! Part II (p. 28) (Student answers will vary.)

A. 1. It was used as a scarecrow to protect the crops. It was a god or representation of a god and used to ensure a good crop.

   2. The stake it was attached to, crops in rows, barn

   3. They knew how to farm. They were not very scientific. (They may have depended on the statue's presence for good crops.) They may have believed in nature gods.

B. 1. The statue was possibly used for protection, as a fertility god, or perhaps as a child's doll.

   2. The bed

   3. They were superstitious. They may have believed that the statue would protect them while they were sleeping. They may have believed that the statue would help them produce children. They may have believed in allowing their children to sleep with their toys.

C. 1. The rocks were used as an altar or a barbecue.

   2. The logs and the animal skeleton

   3. They could have been superstitious. They raised or hunted animals for food and clothing.

D. 1. The rocks were used to make a kiln.

   2. The various pots and bowls, the potter's wheel

   3. They knew how to fire clay. They were artists. They knew how to make wheels.

Midden Questions (p. 32)

A. 1. People ate candy, vegetables (list kinds), meat (list kinds), fruit, cereal, bread, milk and dairy products

2. Most were not farmers.

3. Most of the food was packaged in containers. Some food had already been prepared: cheese, orange juice, cereal, candy bars

4. Yes. There were some farmers in their society.

5. Because food was being sold in large quantities, a surplus of food was being produced. This cannot occur without farming.

6. Some food was prepared in factories by workers. People also prepared food at home.

7. The wrappers and labels were printed by machine and sealed by machine. Food portions are in standard sizes; cans were sealed by machine. Ingredients are present, but there are no pre-prepared meals.

B.

SITEM	POSSIBLE INFORMATION THAT COULD BE LEARNED ABOUT THE SOCIETY
candy bars	liked sweets, ate sweets regularly, knew how to grow and process chocolate, traded for chocolate
frozen vegetables	knew the importance of eating vegetables, knew how to make plastic, understood the process of preserving foods by freezing, knew how to read and write
canned vegetables	knew how to preserve foods, used pounds and ounces as units of measure, knew how to mine and process metals
ice cream carton	raised animals for milk, liked cold desserts, used ground wood to make paper products, used chemical flavorings and colorings, had individual refrigeration systems (freezer)
meats	raised animals for food, raised animals in mass quantities, had computers and laser scanners, used money
fruit and vegetables	ate fresh fruit and vegetables
cereal box	added sugar and fat to their products, grew grain, listed the ingredients on their packages
bread wrapper	bread was baked in large bakeries, yeast was used in the bread
milk cartons	added vitamins to their milk, understood how to kill germs by pasteurization, knew that germs caused disease
orange juice	extracted the juice from the fruit, knew how to concentrate liquids

Midden Practice Part I (p. 33)

1. They ate fruit, shellfish, and insects. They drank milk. They ate stews flavored with peppers. They roasted their food by skewering it on sticks and holding it over an open flame.

2. Yes. Most were farmers.

3. There is evidence of trade. Reasoning: They could not obtain shellfish from a long distance without trading for them. In order to trade, they must have had surplus food to trade, or surplus

food allowed some members of the society to spend their time making other goods for trade.

4. No. Most were farmers.

5. They must have domesticated animals so that they could collect milk from them.

6. They prepared their food.

7. There is no evidence that the food was prepared by others. There are pots and shells and cooking sticks that indicate that they did their own cooking.

ITEM	POSSIBLE INFORMATION THAT COULD BE LEARNED ABOUT THE SOCIETY
watermelon rinds	ate raw fruit, ate without silverware
orange rinds	drank orange juice, made sharp knives
shellfish shells	ate shellfish, traded with people who lived near the ocean, had a good transportation system
gourds	liked music, had time to paint
rings of flowers	wore flowers in their hair or around their necks
pottery pitcher	knew how to fire pottery, raised animals for milk, drank milk or used it in cooking
insect parts	ate the bodies of insects after removing their wings and legs, ate food gathered in the wild
bag with peppers	knew how to weave cloth, raised peppers, used peppers to season their food
clay pots	cooked over open flames, made food in huge quantities, cooked communally
sharpened sticks	cooked food by skewering it on sticks and holding them over an open flame, no silverware—probably ate with their fingers

Midden Practice Part II (p. 34)

1. They ate meats and vegetables. They made some of their food. They caught fish and hunted animals for food. They also ate many meals that were completely prepared. They threw away a lot of non-recyclable things.

2. No. Most were not farmers.

3. There is little evidence of fresh, non-processed food.

4. Yes. Only some were farmers in their society.

5. A farmer had to grow the grain from which the flour was made, the tomatoes and spices from which the red sauce was made, the potatoes, and the grapes from which the wine was made. In addition, the fact that there are many items that are produced by specialized labor suggest a surplus food supply which in turn indicates agriculture.

6. Factories, fast-food establishments, and the people themselves prepared their food.

7. There were printed packages, fast food paper wrappers and bags, and the kettle.

ITEM	POSSIBLE INFORMATION THAT COULD BE LEARNED ABOUT THE SOCIETY
fish line, fish heads	ability to manufacture chemical products like nylon, ability to catch fish, didn't eat fish heads, ate fish
flour and yeast	raised grain, made flour in large quantities, ate bread, made paper, had printing presses
deer bones	ate animal meat, did not use the bones, knew how to hunt
wine bottles	knew how to make glass, drank alcoholic beverages, knew how to ferment grapes, raised grapes, did not recycle
broken toys, birthday paper	played with toys, toys were made in factories, knew how to build boats, gave gifts on birthdays, celebrated birthdays
potato peels	ate many potatoes, did not eat the peels, grew potatoes
kettle	knew how to mine and form metals, cooked their meals
paper and pencils	many people knew how to write, knew how to make paper and pencils, people were educated
fast food papers	some people made their living by preparing food for others, ate many meals prepared by others, knew how to make paper
paper plates	used disposable plates, grew tomatoes, did not recycle paper

Burial Sites Part I (p. 37) (Possible Answers)

1. Each skeleton held a candle to light the way to the afterlife.

2. The clay jars contained valuables to buy their way into heaven. The designs on them also served as a map to heaven.

3. Yes. These people believed in an afterlife. There are really only two reasons that people place items in graves with dead people. One reason is to show people later how wonderful the person had been while they were alive. The other reason is to provide the person with things that he or she can take to use in the afterlife. The jewels, coins, candle, and clay jar do not seem to suggest the first reason. Therefore, their presence seems to show that these people believed in an afterlife.

4. They believed people went to the North Star when they died.

5. The child's hand holding the woman's hand meant that children were buried with their mothers, or a woman was needed to lead a child to the afterlife, or perhaps the child led the women to the afterlife.

6. Women were facing the North Star so that their spirits would be facing in the correct direction when they awoke.

7. The men were positioned to be subservient to the women (at least in this regard). Women were probably the religious leaders and possibly also the political leaders of their society. The women seem to lead the men to the afterlife.

8. The hands of many of the men were touching the foot of a woman so the men would not be lost in their journey to the afterlife.

9. It appears that girls were not considered adults until the age of twelve and therefore were not considered capable of leading others to the afterlife. In addition, they may also have been considered innocent children who had done no wrong and did not need jewels to buy their entrance into the afterlife. They automatically knew how to find their way to the afterlife without a map.

Burial Sites Part II (p. 38) (Possible Answers)

1. The pit was placed inside the cave to keep out wild animals or human enemies or evil spirits.

2. The bodies were placed inside the cave to protect their spirits from evil supernatural beings (gods?). They may also have believed that the bodies needed to be unharmed by predators so that they could enter the afterlife.

3. The faces of the skeletons were covered with masks because they were afraid of supernatural being(s) and they did not want them to know who they were. The masks were either a disguise or to scare the being(s) away.

4. They may have believed that the spirits would be able to see the evil god(s) better if the eyes were larger. They may also have believed that it was dark in the afterlife and they would need large eyes so that they could see.

5. These people put weapons in the hands of the dead so that their spirits could protect themselves. Perhaps they needed to fight their way to the afterlife.

6. Yes. These people believed in an afterlife. There are really only two reasons that people place items in graves with dead people. One reason is to show people later how wonderful the person had been while they were alive. The other reason is to provide the person with things that he or she can take with them to use in the afterlife. The weapons, masks, and musical instruments do not seem to fit the first reason and therefore must show that these people believed in an afterlife.

7. These people believed that they would stay in the cave. The bodies were lying in defensive positions as if they would never move.

8. The bodies were facing toward the cave so that the rock would protect them from being attacked from the back and also so they could talk to each other.

9. The females were placed on one side of the cave and the males were placed on the other because these people did not seem to have family units and males lived independently of females.

10. The musical instruments were provided so that the people could play them after they had died. They may also have been provided to bring them comfort. Their afterlife seems frightening and lonely.

Reading the Bones Part I (p. 41)

Skeleton B 1. Male

        2. About 60 inches, or 5 ft.

        3. 6–8 years old

Skeleton C 1. Female

        2. About 62 inches, or 5 ft. 2 in.

        3. 14–15 years old

Reading the Bones Part II (p. 42)

Skeleton D 1. Female

        2. The skull is smaller and more triangular.

        3. About 52 inches, or 4 ft. 4 in.

        4. 19–20 years

        5. By looking at the places where the bones had stopped growing.

Skeleton E 1. Male

        2. The head is larger and more square.

        3. About 69 inches, or 5 ft. 8 in.

        4. 17–18 years old

        5. By looking at the places where the bones had stopped growing.

American Culture Mind Map #4 (p. 47)

(Possible Answers to #3 Bubbles, entered into #4 bubbles as arranged on p. 46)

CUSTOMS

1. What holiday customs do Americans have? Dye eggs at Easter, buy new clothes at Easter, decorate Christmas trees, exchange gifts at Christmas and Hanukkah, eat turkey and stuffing for Thanksgiving, stay up until midnight and have parades to celebrate the New Year, light fireworks on the Fourth of July.

2. What is the most common mode of transportation? Car, truck.

3. How do Americans dress? Women wear pants, dresses, or skirts and blouses. Men wear suits, long pants, ties, slacks, and shirts. Both men and women wear blue jeans and T-shirts when dressing casually.

4. What are the American habits involving food and eating? Americans eat three meals each day—breakfast soon after getting up in the morning, lunch around noon, and dinner in the early evening. They sit in chairs around a table. They eat with forks, knives, and spoons made of metal. They usually use paper napkins, but may occasionally use cloth ones. Americans eat a lot of fast food like hamburgers, hot dogs, french fries, tacos, and pizza.

5. How do Americans spend their free time? Watch television; read books and magazines; play sports like soccer, football, volleyball, softball; go to movies; attend concerts; play in the park; go to amusement parks; listen to music

6. What kind of houses do people live in? Houses are generally made of stucco, wood, or brick and are rectangular. Some are for one family and some are for many families. Most families consist of mother, father, and their children.

ATTITUDES

1. What is the American attitude toward the government? Many feel it is the best government in the world, they think taxes are too high, they feel free to complain about it, they think the government will protect them and take care of them.

2. How do Americans feel about education? They believe every child is entitled to a free education, they think that school is important.

3. What are American attitudes toward the environment? Many believe that wild areas like national parks should be saved, people should protect endangered animals, people should not litter, people should recycle, people should not pollute the air and water.

4. How do Americans feel about war? They think that sometimes war is necessary. They will fight to defend their freedom. They will fight to defend the freedom of another country.

ART

1. What kinds of music/ musicians have Americans created? Jazz, rhythm and blues, disco, new wave, Elvis

2. What kind of art/ artists have Americans created? Georgia O'Keefe, Grandma Moses, Frederic Remington, instant photographs, Andrew Wyeth

3. Which writers and poets have made America famous? Walt Whitman, Mark Twain, O. Henry, Ernest Hemingway

ACHIEVEMENTS

1. What are some famous American inventions? Radio, television, sewing machine, car, assembly line, microwave oven

2. What achievements have Americans made in medicine? Salk polio vaccine, doctor's offices, X-ray and MRI machines, hospitals, medical schools

3. What have Americans accomplished in science? Space shuttle, trip to the moon, Hubble telescope, computers, telephones connecting every building, refrigerators, dishwashers, electric lights, dams and power plants, ballpoint pen, toilets

4. What is American government like? America is a republic. The President and members of congress are voted in by the people. Americans have a Constitution and a Bill of Rights.

BELIEFS

1. What do people believe about religion? Some people worship God in churches; others do not. Many Americans believe that religion should be a personal choice.

2. What do Americans believe about freedom? Many Americans believe that freedom is good but requires some restraints. For example, government must make laws that citizens abide by. Wars are fought in the name of freedom.

3. What do people believe about death? Americans bury, burn, and sometimes embalm the dead. It is a show of respect. Keeping ashes allows loved ones to hold on to something tangible. Americans remember the dead with grave markers and flowers.

Artifacts and Culture (p. 50) (Possible Answers)

1. They create different kinds of music (Art). They like to listen to different kinds of music (Custom). They have harnessed electricity, developed electronics, manufactured plastic (Achievement). They think that people should have a choice in the music they listen to (Attitude).

2. They think that people should not eat foods with fat (Attitude). They believe people should be thin (Attitude). They eat prepackaged foods (Custom). They know how to manufacture aluminum (or steel) cans and cardboard boxes (Achievement).

3. Some people attend church (Custom). They have unique architecture in their churches like a domed roof and stained glass windows (Art). They believe in freedom of religion or at least a choice of churches (Belief).

4. They think that people should have laws to follow (Attitude). They believe that people should have a voice in their government (Belief). They know how to make paper (Achievement). They have a written language (Achievement).

Culture of the Dig (p. 52)

ACHIEVEMENTS: knew how to weave cloth, knew how to use natural things to make dyes, developed a system of writing, recorded important events in their society, knew how to make boats, learned how to weave baskets from grasses

CUSTOMS: followed the path to the ocean often; swam or bathed in the ocean often; the swim or bath was ritualistic; placed shells by a person's house to show courageous deeds or a record number of fish caught (the more shells, the more prestigious the person); ate shellfish, grains and seaweed; made clothing of tan cloth; went fishing; everyone in the village ate fish

BELIEFS: believed that red was a sacred color to be worn only at burial, worshipped dolphins, did not believe in eating mammals, believed that they became dolphins when they died, only the religious leader of the village could weave the red cloth

ATTITUDES: writing was sacred, not everyone should learn to read and write, the writing was kept by the leader of the tribe, everyone in the village was expected to do their share of the work, they did not use weapons to harm animals, they did not fight other humans, fighting was wrong, recreation and playing was important

ART: created patterns in their baskets and cloth, carved wood, created colors of cloth by blending dyes, made art that was practical

Stable Food Supply (p. 58)

1. Agriculture is the planting of crops and the raising of animals useful to humans.

2. Hunter-gatherers are people who obtain food by hunting wild animals and gathering wild vegetables, fruits, and nuts. They move constantly in search of new food supplies.

3. The agricultural tribes finished their projects first.

4. The other tribes had trouble finishing their projects because the hunter-gatherer tribes had to spend too much time gathering food.

5. The agricultural tribe is more likely to build large towns.

   Hunter-gatherers need to be able to move to follow the food supply. It is more difficult to move a large town.

6. The agricultural tribe is more likely to come up with new inventions.

   They don't have to spend all of their time finding food because they plant their plants and raise their animals near their homes.

7. In an agricultural tribe, everyone doesn't need to gather food because agriculture allows for a surplus of food. That means that not everyone has to grow their own food. Those who don't spend their time growing food can use their time to build the town.

8. Object B might have been found in a hunter-gatherer village.

9. Object A might have been found in an agricultural village.

10. In an agricultural village, people would not have to move around to find food so they would have time to create sculptured vases like the one in A. Inhabitants of a hunter-gatherer tribe would use simple stone bowls to grind the seeds they found because they would not have to spend as much time making them.

11. Object C might have been found in a hunter-gatherer village.

12. Objects A and B might have been found in an agricultural village.

13. In an agricultural village, not all of the people need to raise food. People have time to spend on other interests such as the writing and architecture shown in A and B. The people in a hunter-gatherer village are primarily concerned with collecting food. Most of their tools were for gathering food. They were simple like the spear in picture C.

Domestication #1 (p. 60)

Wheat Seed Numbers: 3, 7, 12, 13, 14, 20

Wild		Domestic	
Seed #	Length	Seed #	Length
12	10 mm.	3	12 mm.
13	5 mm.	7	12 mm.
		14	13 mm.
		20	18 mm.
Total Length: 15 mm.		Total Length: 55 mm	
Average: 7.5 mm.		Average: 13.75 mm.	

Pumpkin Seed Numbers: 2, 5, 9, 10, 11, 15, 17, 18

Wild		Domestic	
Seed #	Length	Seed #	Length
5	6 mm.	2	13 mm.
9	6 mm.	11	18 mm.
10	7 mm.	15	12 mm.
		17	12 mm.
		18	16 mm.
Total Length: 19 mm.		Total Length: 71 mm.	
Average: 6.3 mm.		Average: 14.2 mm.	

Corn Seed Numbers: 1, 4, 6, 8, 16, 19, 21

Wild		Domestic	
Seed #	Length	Seed #	Length
1	8 mm.	6	11 mm
4	8 mm.	8	12 mm
19	6 mm.	16	13 mm
		21	10 mm
Total Length: 22 mm.		Total Length: 46 mm.	
Average: 7.3 mm.		Average: 11.5 mm.	

Domestication #2—Seeds (p. 61)

A.

1. The total number of seeds in box A is 21.

2. The total number of domestic seeds of all types is 13.

3. The total number of wild seeds of all types is 8.

4. The total number of domestic seeds divided by the total number of seeds is 0.62

5. The total number of wild seeds divided by the total number of seeds is 0.38

6. 223

7. 137

8. See graph

B.

1. This society was mostly agricultural.

2. There were more seeds from domestic plants than from wild plants.

3. The wild pumpkin seeds in box A became the size of the domestic seeds because people chose the largest of the wild seeds and used them to plant in a garden. Next year, the people chose the largest seeds from that crop and kept them to plant in the garden the following year. This process continued until the seeds were the size of the domestic ones.

4. These people were farmers. They did not have to migrate to find new sources of food or to follow migrating herds of animals.

Four Walls (p. 65)

Upper Left

1. Rough, odd-shaped stones, probably picked up from surrounding area

2. Stones, hands

3. None

4. People with a low level of technology. Few or no tools were used. The stones were probably found. The wall could have been built by one person.

Lower Left

1. Straight, even bricks

2. Bricks, mortar, trowel, bucket, level

3. How to make bricks, how to work metal to make trowel and level, how to make a bucket

4. Brick factory workers, truckers, metal workers, trowel factory workers, level factory workers, bucket makers

Upper Right

1. Plastic wall with grooves

2. Plastic, molds, factory full of machines, screwdriver, hammer

3. How to make plastic, how to smelt metal into machines, how to make machines

4. Truck drivers, plastic mixers and pourers, scrapers, cleaners, machine operators, miners, metal machine factory workers, etc.

Lower Right

1. Odd-shaped bricks, probably handmade

2. Mud, wood frame, straw

3. How to mix the mud and straw, how to make bricks

4. Person who gathered the wood, farmer who raised the straw, brick maker

Level of Technology—Transportation (p. 66)

A. Leather, bow and arrow (or gun), needle

How to tan leather, how to sew

B. Metal, plastic, rubber, fabric, glass, hammers, screwdrivers, welding tools, sewing machine, screws, glue

How to mine and manufacture metal, how to make plastic, rubber, and glass, how to weave fabric.

C. Metal, plastic, glass, electronics, screws, screwdrivers, welding tools

How to mine and manufacture metal, how things fly (aerodynamics), how to make plastic, rubber, glass, electronic instruments

D. Wood, carving knife, axe or saw

How to carve wood, how to make a boat that will float, how to make oars

1. C, B, D, A

2. C required the most tools, material, knowledge, and skills. B required less than C. D required less than B, but more than A. A required the least.

3. They did not have the tools, materials, knowledge, or skills to build an airplane.

Specialization of Labor Diagram—Clock (p. 67) (Diagram answers will vary. See example on page 64.)

1. Possibly 18 if they filled in each box.

2. They get their food from grocery stores, which get the food from the farmers.

3. High

4. Hunter-gatherer societies are too busy hunting and gathering food to do anything else.

5. The domestication of food and animals allows people more time. They do not have to travel from place to place in search of food.

The King's House (p. 71)

1. Drawings will vary.

2. The walls are a variety of different sizes, styles, and colors.

3. A model of the wall could have been built first by one person. Then everyone could work together to make it look like the model. One person could have handed out instructions to everyone else before building.

4. Government

5. Drawings should be similar.

6. This house stands up. All the parts look alike. It looks like there was a plan.

7. The street is straight. The entire length is made of the same material. It is the same width for the entire length.

8. The street starts and stops at different places. Different sections are made in a different way using different materials. Various sections are of different widths and were built at different times.

Government Projects (p. 73)

Box A should be labeled "without a government." Box B should be labeled "with a government." Drawings will vary.

1. A project that is done by the government is usually large. It shows that a lot of people worked on the project. Planning is apparent in the consistency of the size, materials, and construction of the project.

2. The project is too large. Someone would need to pay for the project and it is too expensive for one person to pay for. Someone needed to provide food (or money for food) for the people who worked on the project.

3. It is large. It requires a lot of people to build it. It needs to be organized by someone. It is expensive. Someone needed to provide food for the people that worked on the project.

4. Smaller artifacts. Pieces that are different. Answers may vary.

5. Large artifacts. Pieces that are all alike. Answers may vary.

Hometown (p. 74)

Part II

1. Answers will vary, but should include something about assigning more people to defend Hometown.

2. Answers will vary, but should include something about being unable to complete other jobs because rival towns (the teacher) kept ruining or stealing the products of their work.

3. The town was defended and little or no problems were caused by rival towns.

4. Fewer people were able to do the work in the town—plant crops, build streets, buildings, and walls, etc.

5. In order to survive and grow, a civilization must be protected from being attacked and/or taken over by another civilization.

6. Assign a large number of people to defense. Choose a location that is protected from other civilizations by natural barriers such as mountains, rivers, oceans, and deserts.

Government Defenses (p. 77)

Part I

Locations will vary. Reasons should include some of the following:

1. Placed the civilization as far from other people as possible.

2. Placed the civilization on the other side of the river from Freeville.

3. Placed the civilization on the other side of the desert from Freeville.

4. Placed the civilization on the other side of the mountains from Freeville.

5. Placed the civilization on the plain so that it would have good farming land.

6. Placed the civilization near the ocean so it would provide transportation and food.

7. Placed the civilization near the river so that there would be water to drink and to feed crops.

8. Placed the civilization near the river so that the river would provide transportation.

Part II

Artifacts may vary, but should include large defense projects. Some examples might be a large moat or wall around the entire village, a large defense weapon like a catapult, large numbers of identical uniforms or small weapons, lookout towers, or a military base.

Your Radiocarbon Cycle Diagram— Shoelace (p. 85) (Answers may vary. Accept anything reasonable.)

1. The sun's energy hits the earth.

2. Nitrogen atoms are turned into radiocarbon.

3. Radiocarbon joins with oxygen to form carbon dioxide.

4. The grass takes in carbon dioxide made with radiocarbon.

5. A cow eats grass containing the radiocarbon atom.

6. While the cow is alive, the number of radiocarbon atoms being introduced remains equal to the number undergoing decay to nitrogen.

7. A man kills the cow and makes a shoelace from the leather. The radiocarbon levels start to decrease.

8. Archaeologists find the leather shoelace. They subtract the number of radiocarbon atoms remaining from the number of radiocarbon atoms the cow possessed when it was alive to determine the age of the shoelace.

Radiocarbon Decay (p. 87) (Example)

1. There are millions of cars in our country.

2. Each car has a tank full of gas.

3. Every time a car's tank gets low on gas, the owner fills it with more gas. This continues as long as there is more gas.

4. If there were no more gas, one car would run out of gas and stop running.

5. As time passed, more cars would run out of gas and stop running.

6. After a time, all of the cars would run out of gas and stop running.

Transparency—Radiocarbon Dating (p. 88)

1. No. It was never alive.

2. Yes. It is made out of wood, which was once alive. It is between 1000 and 50,000 years old.

3. Yes. It is made out of leather from a cow, which was once alive. It is between 1000 and 50,000 years old.

4. No. It is made from plastic and man-made materials. It is less than 1000 years old.

5. No. The metal was never alive.

6. Yes. It is made of cotton, which was once alive.

Radiocarbon Dating—Artifacts (p. 89)

Part I

Place an X next to items 2, 3, 4, 10, 11, and 12.

Part II

(Paragraphs should include the following information.)

1. Dinosaur bones are too old to be dated using the radiocarbon dating method.

5. A living tree is too young to be dated using the radiocarbon dating method.

6. Glass was never alive and cannot be dated using the radiocarbon dating method.

7. A copper spoon is made from metal, which was never alive.

8. Stone arrowheads were never alive.

9. A book published in 1994 is too new to be dated using the radiocarbon dating method.

Counting the Years (p. 90)

1. 7872 years

2. 8814 years

3. 5698 years

4. 9562 years